SIMPLICITY

GEORGES LEFEBVRE O.S.B.

SIMPLICITY

The Heart of Prayer

translated by
DINAH LIVINGSTONE

Foreword by
SIMON TUGWELL O.P.

PAULIST PRESS

New York/Paramus/Toronto

Published by arrangement with Darton, Longman and Todd, Ltd., 85 Gloucester Road, London SW7 4SU.

Originally published as *Simplicité de la Prière* by Desclée de Brouwer, Paris and © 1974.

ISBN: 0-8091-1881-5

Cover Design: Dan Pezza

Published by Paulist Press
Editorial Office: 1865 Broadway, N.Y., N.Y. 10023
Business Office: 400 Sette Drive, Paramus, N.J. 07652

Printed in the United States of America

CONTENTS

FOREWORD

'But what is the secret of finding this treasure, this mustard seed, this drachma? There is no secret at all. The treasure is everywhere, it offers itself to us at every moment, in every place.' How busily man seeks and struggles to find some place of repose for himself, some little sense of fulfilment, of meaning, of achievement! And how little he finds for all his toil. How he wrestles to understand the mystery of his own heart, to decipher the curious yearnings and dissatisfactions that he finds there! Why is it that he so often ends up tired and disillusioned, capable finally only of killing time with thrillers and tranquillisers?

Is it not perhaps that we have forgotten that oldest, most courteous of arts, the art of receiving? Perhaps religious people most of all, haunted by what is almost a scruple about the need to do things for God and man, to do something commensurate with the gift we still know we have received from God, have forgotten that the only sacrifice we can really offer to God is to receive the cup of salvation from His loving hand (Psalm 115).

In this beautiful book by Dom Georges Lefebvre, we are invited to rediscover the essential simplicity of prayer, in rediscovering the simplicity of life, of faith. 'It is not necessary,' he tells us, 'to see clearly all that is in our heart for us to offer it simply in a gesture of confidence. To believe peacefully that we are loved: that is still true, even if we do not seem able to feel it. That which is most true in us is hidden in the deepest place of our heart. To guess its secret, we must not violate it.'

There is no need to carry over into our prayer the hectic quality of modern life, nor the desperate need to succeed, to prove ourselves, to be conscious of where and who we are. These meditations can help us to rest in that cradle of love which is the source of all that we are and do: 'the eternal God is your dwelling place, and underneath are the everlasting arms' (Deuteronomy 33.27.). They are as convincing an exposition as I have ever seen of what pure, living faith means. It means that God loves me, and that that is enough. In a way both deeply theological and wisely human, Dom Lefebvre brings us back to the centre, to the one thing needful. In so far as we learn to see things aright, in their true perspective, it will be difficult for us not to pray.

Simon Tugwell, O.P.

Oxford
September 22, 1974

PART ONE

The Heart of Prayer

1. GOD IS LOVE

At the centre of our christian faith stands the sacrifice of the cross. There God reveals his love for us in an action which is a deep mystery of humility.

It is the sign we have been given and to which we must look if we are to recognise our God, the true God and seek his face.

If we think about ourselves truthfully, we realise we are poor and weak. We see that we are constricted by limitations which seem all the more hampering because we want to overcome them, to go beyond ourselves.

But how can we go beyond ourselves? One possibility is self-aggrandisement and domination, the will to power over ourselves and others. A noble ambition, perhaps, but vitiated by the pride which is at its root and supplies its strength.

In its most extreme form it leads to the sin of Satan, delight in one's own perfection, desiring to possess it quite independently, refusing to bow down to anyone or recognise any master. It is setting oneself above others, forcing them to submit, demanding the honour due to God alone.

This sin usurps God's grandeur for does not his infinite majesty consist precisely in his inalienable possession as his own by right of this infinite fulness of perfection, dignity and power, which no one else can lay claim to without sacrilegious pride?

If we are told that God expects something from us other than submission and reverence, that he asks us to love him, can these words have any real meaning for us? Can the truth of these words really be true to us? God condescends to invite us to intimate friendship with himself in his majesty and power, but how can such a relationship really be intimate? He is merciful but when he looks down on us can it really be with love? With kindness, yes, but with love? Is it possible for two beings so far apart really to love one another?

A great love

No, if God is love, truly, and asks us to love him, he must be different from the majestic image we tremblingly form of him. Certainly he is great, but his greatness is not at all like our human greatnesses, our dreams of ambition and power. His greatness is quite different from the ambition and pride of Satan, who thought he was imitating God and making himself like him!

God's greatness is far richer and more mysterious. It has an inexhaustible fulness because God is love and his is the greatness of love. It is not like ours, a barren greatness seeking to impose itself, strictly demanding its due, and self-centred in its affirmation of power.

God's greatness is simple and quite free from the pride which mars all human greatness. It is infinitely simple, and if we can imagine what it might mean to use the word of God, infinitely humble.

His greatness is accessible and infinitely near. God loves us. He loves us as Jesus Christ loved Peter the faithful and upright servant, and John his favourite disciple, and Lazarus and Mary and the children who were brought to him, and his mother.

God the Father of heaven, who reigns from age to age, also loves us: 'Have I been with you so long, and yet you do not know me, Philip? He who has seen me has seen the Father; how can you say, "Show us the Father"?' (Jn. 14.9.).

God loves us. He has told us this plainly enough in scripture, the long education he gave his chosen people, leading them from the first revelation of the Lord before whom all the earth trembles to the full light of Christ, God made man for the love of mankind.

Should we take more notice of philosophers' speculations and the glimmerings of light they offer us than of the simple evidence of every page of the gospel?

God loves us truly. His love is the truest love of all; it is the only real love, which truly and fully possesses real love's characteristics. It is closer and more intimate than any other love.

This is not because he stoops so low to love us but because of what the divine nature is. God loves us because he is love, because he is by nature fulness of giving and communion.

To make plain the meaning of what we say when we say that God is love, perhaps we should also say that God is humility. We have to be clear that we are not using the word humility in the usual way when we use it of God, but isn't that true of all the words we use of God?

Love's humility
So what is humility? Pride is selfishness which hangs on to what it has, and is shut in upon itself. Humility on the other hand gives freely of what it has, makes it openly available to all. Such generosity is the first condition for communion with others.

God has perfect freedom to give himself. He possesses all that he has, all that he is, his infinite perfection in complete freedom. This is his nature. This is what we mean when we say that God is love.

We must not belittle or confine this divine liberty by imposing our petty ideas of greatness on it. 'Though he was in the form of God [he] did not count equality with God a thing to be grasped, but emptied himself, taking the form of a servant, being born in the likeness of men' (Ph. 2.6-7.).

God does not hang on jealously to his greatness – it is not that kind of greatness – and if he asks us to give him the homage that is his due, this means first of all recognising his true nature, which he has deigned to reveal to us, recognising his boundless love in all its fulness, its infinite simplicity and freedom.

We cannot approach this love except by humility. We must shake off the bonds of selfishness, become free of the hardening effects of pride. Gradually the experience of our poverty and nothingness must lead us to detachment, self-effacement, the giving up to self, and towards love, humble love. (That is why chastity is in such close harmony with charity. We see this more clearly when we realise that it is a form of humility, the opposite of 'the pride of the flesh'. It is part of the self effacement which prepares us to receive God's love as a free gift, infinitely pure and delicate.)

The sign of the cross
God came to us by the way of the cross. And this is the way he invites us to go to him. We try to understand the mystery if his life in which humility and love are so closely connected.

It is the way of the cross which leads us to the heart of the divine mystery, where in the end there is as much joy in giving as in receiving, because both are ways of entering into the same communion.

Both require freedom from self, freedom to give without holding anything back, and freedom to receive God's gift and live by it. His grace is completely free and we must allow it to imbue us with its own generosity and free communion.

This is the only way we can escape our own limitations, and

reach God, not to snatch his greatness from him, but to commune with him in his generous love, in the divine mystery where love and humility – in the deepest and most godlike sense of the word – are but one.

We live by this love, it dwells in our hearts but it is deeper than our hearts. It has all the mystery of God himself; it is a close communion with God and its secret is not revealed until we see him face to face in heaven. We live by it through faith. It is a hidden reality; we only feel that it fills us, and glimpse some of its immensity as we learn to lose ourselves in God.

Love's justice

The philosophers call God transcendent because he is fulness of being. He exists of himself in sovereign independence. Faith sees God's transcendence in this: that created being turned in on itself can only be confined within the narrow limits of its own selfishness, but in God's infinity there is room to spread out in love. God in himself enjoys infinite loving. This is the secret of the inner life of the Trinity.

We stand before this mystery. We are called to a supernatural vocation which brings us into communion with this mystery of love.

Of course it is true to say that God is infinite justice. But we should not think of love and justice as two distinct attributes side by side, the one setting limits to the other, each with its own requirements which have to be reconciled. Love and justice are united as one. But the notion of justice is narrower than that of love. Its point of view is more limited, and that is why it more easily distorts our view and leads to wrong conclusions. Justice which was nothing but justice would not be God's justice.

But love is a wider notion, it includes justice but goes beyond it. It places justice in a wider context and so gives it a truer meaning. We shall never understand God's justice – which goes beyond all our human ideas of justice – unless we realise that it goes together with his love. God's justice is still his love.

Justice is truth: it is respect for the truth of things. God is just because he respects the truth of his love. If we are to commune in his mystery, he requires us to come before him in the truth.

When we realise this many things in the life of the spirit become simpler and clearer.

Our faith's response

We respond first and foremost by prayer, knowing that we are really in the presence of this mystery of love, not just 'the love of God', as we call it, but love which is God. God's infinite light streams with the power of giving, of communion. We must believe with a firm enough faith not to be dismayed by any darkness. We should not worry if we feel nothing in our prayer of an attitude of mind befitting so great a mystery. We must believe in God's transcendence and not think that its power is diminished by our inability to realise it. We must have faith in this mystery of love, believe that it does not depend on what we see of it, but that it is all our hope and always there.

Faith enables us to receive its life giving force – humble faith which is all adoration and recognition of its infinite fulness. By this humble faith we know that in accepting emptiness, the desert and the darkness, simply and peacefully we bear witness to the mystery's transcendence, and stand before it in the truth.

This is what our prayer should express: our humble adoration of the infinite fulness of divine love, faith in the boundless fulness of this love which has taken us on and does its work in us, our longing to open ourselves completely to it and put no obstacle in its way. We should have an attitude of openness, of glad and confident welcome. Our welcome has the sweetness of knowing we are loved.

A love present everywhere

Our whole lives should be a response to this love. We should become aware of being in the presence of this mystery, a living and personal mystery, in the presence of someone who loves us deeply, tenderly and kindly. Then we should do all we can to make all our lives a response to this love, the only response expected of us, a total act of faith.

If we were really aware of being in the presence of this great mystery of love, it would affect all our reactions to all the little events of every day. This love is deep and full, it is God himself. If we believed in it with true faith we would confidently accept everything that happened, and our trust would be full of respect and adoration. Many feelings would no longer find room in our hearts. They would be at variance with what was deepest in us. We might still suffer, but we should no longer feel bitter or aggrieved. We would look at things peacefully and kindly; we would be saved the feverish exaggerations of selfishness.

Nothing matters beside this love which leads us, this mystery which enfolds and penetrates all our lives.

The only way of seeing things that happen round us with true sympathy is to believe with true faith that they are part of what God's love wants for us, the ways by which he leads us, he is present in them all and gives himself to us in this way.

He is present everywhere even in the shortcomings of people who hurt us – and in our own. These shortcomings are not ours and theirs, they are the common weakness of humanity and belong to us all. Our own weakness makes us share in this human poverty, makes us part of it.

If we fixed our eyes on the mystery of God's love, if we recognised it *in* this human weakness, we should no longer see this weakness as love's enemy. We could see it as the poverty towards which God stoops in his mercy, the fulness of his revelation – 'et misericordia eius super omnia opera eius'. It is this weakness towards which he is merciful, in which he is at work, reveals himself, offers himself to us and asks us to recognise him.

We share in this human wretchedness as we also share in the mystery of love which is enacted in it.

2. THE SOURCES OF PRAYER

Every christian is drawn towards prayer. Even if we do not know how to concentrate on it for any length of time, we feel that it is important, that we should like to pray, that it would be a good and joyful thing bringing us deep peace to live more in the presence of God.

But if we want to reach this state wouldn't it be best to start by trying to rid ourselves of all the inaccurate and perhaps artificial notions we have of prayer? Don't we sometimes continue to hang on more or less consciously to odds and ends of ideas we once accepted uncritically, even if we have now gone beyond them?

No lofty thoughts
For example, 'methods of prayer' are out of fashion, and we should be careful of saying too much against them in case we exaggerate and fail to see what was right about them. But because they suggested that prayer should be a well constructed meditation, a logical process of reflection, this sometimes makes us feel in a muddled way that prayer is principally a mental exercise, turning the mind towards thoughts it must go into deeply and must not be distracted from.

The saints who created these 'methods of prayer' had much less rigid ideas. They regarded these methods as a way of recollection whose end is simple and silent attention to God. A too rigid interpretation of their thought, without due attention to its subtilties was probably what was responsible for the idea – which it is sometimes hard to get away from – that prayer is an intellectual exercise, a work of reflection, a study requiring concentration and the following through of an idea, a careful, conscientious and methodical work.

This is one element of prayer but it is not everything. That would make it too limited and dry.

No ecstasies
But what are the riches of prayer?

There is another mistake to avoid here. If we have read the mystical writers or especially if we have heard them speaking, we might think that according to them, prayer in its highest form consists of fervent emotions, graces overwhelming the soul, with joy, supernatural peace, light transporting the soul to a world where faith already gives way to a kind of vision. Ravishing ecstasies? Are they really the peak of prayer, the proof that it has reached the highest perfection it is capable of? But if we read St Teresa of Avila or St John of the Cross carefully we find that for them God can lead us to the highest perfection without such favours and that even when he sees fit to grant them, they are always merely an intermediate stage which is then superseded by a purer and more secret action of grace which brings true union with God. This is something much humbler and more secret, deeper than all our imaginings.

St John of the Cross says repeatedly that the way of perfection is in the silence of faith, in the inner abandonment of a soul which knows its own poverty and surrenders to God in humility. 'If the soul wants to reach the substance and purity of spiritual good, she must walk the straight short road of dispossession and dryness.'

We also find a significant development in the work of St Teresa. In the *Interior Castle* there is a constant rise until the sixth habitations are reached. These have such a superabundance of supernatural gifts, visions, revelations, ecstasies, ravishments that one wonders what can be left for the seventh. But when these are reached everything goes quiet. There is calm and silence. The soul is compared to Solomon's Temple where no noise was supposed to be heard. Everything has become simple, deep and secret. God scarcely allows the soul to glimpse 'through a little grating' what is happening in its deepest self where he dwells.

And even further on – we refer to the text written four years after the *Interior Castle* – we find that St Teresa's final word on her inner life speaks only of a very simple and deep union with God, in a submission, now almost natural, to all his wishes.

She insists on complete docility and malleability in God's hands. 'My will never opposes, even in its first reaction, the accomplishment of God's will in it.' This takes place in a dispossession of self: 'I am afraid that my soul might be unresponsive and do nothing. I cannot engage in corporal penances. There is no strength in my desire to suffer, to endure martyrdom or see God. Usually

I am incapable of forming such desires.' And finally the astonishing sentence from St Teresa describing the state of her soul when she has reached the peak of mystical life: 'It seems that I live only for the sake of eating and sleeping. I don't worry about anything and even this state does not worry me' (*Eighth Spiritual Relation*).

The simplicity of deep feeling

This is the state of a soul in which grace has gone so deep that it lives with perfect simplicity and spontaneity, its whole self is directed towards God.

This is the perfection of prayer, an attitude of extreme simplicity, an almost unfeeling detachment, of a soul surrendered utterly to God's will. In all things it feels almost naturally that it is not alone but in God's hands, and lets him do what he will with it.

This is the perfection of prayer, a simple, pure and deeply happy but quite unspectacular state. The soul is barely aware of it precisely because it feels so natural. It is with God, it lives with God, it is in God's hands, and remains there of its own accord because it belongs there. It no longer needs all the supports and the aids it used to need to get the feeling of God's presence. It lives by this presence which has penetrated it deeply. The seal of grace is on it, in its deepest self.

Thus we see that the true meaning of prayer comes out better in the expression 'a prayerful soul' than in 'prayer exercises'. When we say 'a prayerful soul' we think of a soul at peace in the way it lives. This is the essence of prayer. This is its goal. When we say 'prayer exercises' we mean certain methods which are used to reach this goal.

A 'prayerful soul' may of course be the result of long labour in which 'prayer exercises' have had a part. But our attitude to these exercises should be determined by their goal, to help us reach a closeness to God, a state in which prayer is 'embodied', to become a truly prayerful soul.

A long association

God draws the soul to him deeply and closely, through graces given, inner graces or external events. The work of grace is a long process. The 'prayerful soul' is the result of this process. When it turns inwards it finds itself in the presence of this long story of its love, just as two friends feel that the bond between them is all their past together, their common memories, all that they have lived through together.

So our prayer becomes a recapitulation of our relations with God, our friendship with him. In it will be contained all the gifts we have received from him in his goodness. These were not a sequence of unconnected favours but a process of grace leading us gradually where it wants us to go. When we receive some new light, it will enhance what has gone before; what has gone before will be contained in it. Every favourite reflection in our prayers is something God has often drawn our attention to, repeatedly stressed. It is part of the secret friendship between us. Grace has ripened it over a long period. And all this increases the feeling of closeness which has grown through living with God, in his presence.

Fulfilment

Prayer fulfils the soul's deepest aspiration. It needs to give itself, which means that it needs God and cannot find rest except in him.

For the human heart cannot find rest in anything limited. If it strays because it has not found the only object worthy of its love, it wanders from pillar to post always unsatisfied, always anxious. This dissatisfaction shows that it was made for something else, for something beyond.

And however much love it may have for anyone or anything, it cannot be satisfied unless it seeks God through this love. God has set the seal of his own love upon it in its deepest self. Loving, real loving can only mean sharing all that is best in you, the need for truth and honesty, the need for an ideal which recognises no limits, but always seeks further, the need for the infinite, the need for God. That is why loving one another is loving God, loving God together.

The light of grace

This is the deepest instinct of our hearts; it may also be the most hidden. But this instinct of our deepest nature is transformed into something higher when it receives the light of grace. Our prayer is taken up into a mystery, the mystery of a presence. Christ said: 'If a man loves me, he will keep my word, and my Father will love him, and we will come to him and make our home with him' (Jn. 14.23.). In Christ we enter into this mystery of communion which is the very life of God. God is present to us in the love which binds the three divine persons in the mystery of the trinity. We are taken up into this mystery by becoming children of God in and with his son. In him and with him we really live with a new life. We are vivified by grace which we can only receive, opening ourselves to it as a gift of love.

Consent

That is why praying is not simply trying to awaken and intensify the need for God which is in our nature, using the faculties we possess by nature. Praying in a deeper sense is opening ourselves to God's grace.

Prayer is consenting to grace. We simply look towards God and say: 'Here I am, I am yours, do what you like with me.'

Prayer is not something we ourselves construct. The object of prayer is not something which will be the result of our own efforts. Essentially it is a welcome to God, a free consent by which we open our soul to him to let him do his will and go along with it as well as we can.

How do we express this consent, this desire? We express it by our efforts to pay attention to God, to turn towards him. We try in all simplicity to do this, using the means we find most helpful to concentration. We never choose a prayer form just because we think it is higher. We must choose the means that best help us to find God modestly and humbly. Thus we will be truthful in our attitude to him. We gladly accept any form of prayer however thin, ordinary and elementary it may seem, as long as it leads us to him. Then our desire will be pure, it will be totally concerned with him we seek without caring whether the ways to him are high or low.

This does not mean agreeing to take the lower way and giving up any thought of reaching the peaks of prayer, content with what he gives us and not asking for more. It means grasping the essential, the real perfection of prayer. We cling all the more closely to God's will when we are humble. It means going to God by the shortest and surest way.

Personal presence

Thus prayer increasingly becomes a true expression of the soul's turning towards God. The soul always and everywhere has the 'feeling' it is not alone. Everything is seen in the light of this dependence on God, this presence in the soul requiring meekness. The soul feels that it is led by the hand, that it is not alone. There is someone watching over it with whom it is in contact. This invisible presence transforms it.

Thus prayer becomes more 'personal'. Gradually the feeling of a close personal relationship grows, the feeling of responding to him who is within us, who is on our side. We receive everything from him and everything in us looks to him.

Prayer is not chiefly reflection but consent. But if we make the effort to remain with God in an attitude of consent, of uniting our wills to his, then without our noticing it we become aware of his presence in our lives – a personal presence. It is like a change of atmosphere, something that just happens. Gradually, without our realising it, through our efforts to pray we become aware of a presence which puts life into these efforts. If we tried to grab it the result might be, in the words of John of the Cross: '... like closing your hand to try and grasp the air in it ... the air escapes.' But if we try simply consenting to God, this itself will lead us to an awareness of his living and personal presence, a friend who is always there.

We must believe what we guess at in the depths of our heart even if we cannot express it very clearly.

Abundant life
This shows clearly that although a true life of prayer needs moments of recollection, of conscious attention to our prayers, it also requires that we try all the time to direct what we do towards God, to submit ourselves to him.

Being faithful to our everyday duties is both a necessary preparation for prayer and, even more, the result of this prayer. Prayer cannot develop and become fully itself unless it has this result. We cannot live by a truly spiritual reality, feel its presence and pay attention to it, unless it affects our everyday lives. Even in human loving, however fond of each other two people are, it does not mean much unless it affects their ordinary lives.

It is the same with the love of God. Even though we have to look deep into our hearts to realise what he means to us, we cannot live by this love except by expressing it in all our doings. This love must be constantly at work in our daily lives, because this is how we live and the atmosphere we live in and the way we become aware of ourselves.

God's love is rooted in our deepest soul, but it is not locked up there and cut off from everything else. It is like a living plant pressing upwards and outwards. It cannot find room to grow unless we give it space in all our doings.

We cannot lead an authentic life of prayer unless this need for God which we have discovered deep within us in our prayer becomes a living reality, everywhere present, a hidden influence which changes everything and gives it new meaning.

In free simplicity

Prayer cannot be present in this way in all our life unless we have a very broad idea of what it is. It is an inner state in which the soul habitually lives, an atmosphere which gradually takes possession of all its attitudes. It must be adaptable, free and sensitive to all the different things that happen, requiring different behaviour.

A prayerful soul remains always in God's presence. Something in it shows that it knows it is in his presence. But this something may sometimes not show very clearly and the undiscerning will not notice it. When we are tired or very busy or worried, we are not the same as when we are quiet and calm. But we should live our faith in God's presence simply and freely, we should seek for signs of his peace clearly and confidently, and breathe the freshness of his atmosphere.

But we should not think of this peace – which results from a 'state' of prayer – as something disembodied, altogether spiritual, belonging to another world and outside everyday life. We should not expect it to be preserved from the vicissitudes of life here below, immune from anxiety or sadness – or even excitement. We find this peace in the circumstances of our daily life, and the impressions these circumstances make on us. In our ordinary human feelings towards ordinary events we discern the presence of this peace which gives them a new colouring. This peace is deeper and truer than all the various impressions which become subject to its kindly influence.

That is why a 'state' of prayer, a continual awareness of God's presence and seeing things in his sight, cannot develop and grow strong except in contact with ordinary life. And if we find it important, and that is up to us, to set aside as much time as we can for prayer, reserved for prayer alone, we should not be surprised that God often puts us in situations where this is difficult and seems to be placing obstacles in our way. Many things can make prayer difficult. Perhaps we are engaged on demanding work, or have some anxiety which stops us concentrating, perhaps our health is not good. But what is asked of us is to bear all this patiently, not to feel desperate as if we were on our own, to persevere as hard as we can, putting ourselves in the hands of grace and letting it lead us where it will and how it will. And our prayer will progress more deeply and truly by this contact with the difficulties of daily life, by this effort to adapt ourselves obediently and confidently to the ways of God, simply accepting what he sends and going forward with him. Grace comes through our daily lives, it is at home there, and that is where it develops and grows normally.

In faith

And if on occasion our struggle either in our daily lives or in spiritual matters becomes really difficult and dismaying, we should remember that this is the heart of the battle taking place in us between grace and the devil.

Grace wants to lead us through the darkness of faith to respond to God's love in the way he expects of us. This effort must be sustained by trust in him alone, by hoping against hope that nothing can daunt our faith. This is the meeting place between the soul freed from selfishness and the infinite freedom of the divine love. But it is also the point where Satan will launch his fiercest attacks; his other victories over us only interest him to the extent that they prepare for his final victory, which will decisively deliver us to him: the act of despair that separates us from God's love and his infinite power to save and redeem us.

And perhaps that is why the darkness encountered by those who seek God with all their hearts has a particular meaning for the communion of saints. This darkness unites us all in the same struggle against the common enemy and we must fight together to unmask his vilest trick which he waits to spring on us in each of his attacks.

3. THE HEART OF PRAYER

St John of the Cross is always writing about 'pure faith', 'living faith'. What does he mean? Sometimes we cannot escape the impression that he is talking about some high faith which is a mystery to us. In fact he describes it as a very pure light, a grace higher than all the others, so that it is worth giving up all other graces in order to live by this faith in a purer way. It is the 'only sure way', 'the best way to go to the goal which is God' (*Ascent of Mount Carmel*, I.2.).

For St John of the Cross this is the most important of all graces because it is the most essential. It is the one thing necessary and the soul which is sincere reckons nothing of any favour which does not strengthen this faith which brings such a close and perfect union with God that the saint says: 'In this life faith brings divine union just as in the other life the light of glory brings the clear vision of God' (*ibid.* 24.).

The first lesson to be drawn from this teaching of the mystical doctor is that the true perfection of prayer is the same thing as what is most essential to prayer. It belongs to the innermost nature of prayer, and so is at the heart of prayer, even the humblest and most elementary prayer, as long as it is true. This is an invitation to search for the treasure in our own field, however poor it may be. The treasure must be there. We must try to recognise it and know its worth.

A dim light

Sometimes for days and days we pray as we can, our prayer is like a little night light which keeps looking as if it is about to go out. We keep wondering whether it has gone out because its light is so feeble it barely pierces the fog of our everyday greyness. But something happens calling for unselfishness on our part, or patient kindness, for example, and we find it has become easier to do it. We are not talking about some momentary fervour, but something at once more real and more secret. We mean something that happens deep down in us connecting us with an experience which overwhelms us more truly and peacefully than ever before and becomes the most valuable thing we know. We must follow this movement in the depths of our hearts and what used to be a struggle causing suffering and resignation becomes quite simple.

Thus the hidden grace and quiet light which have been slowly penetrating us during a period of harsh perseverance in apparently unrewarding prayer, suddenly reveal themselves.

This soft quiet light which is simple and pure and full of love is St John of the Cross's 'pure faith' and 'hidden faith': 'the dark and loving knowledge which is faith' (*ibid.*). If we let it, this light will lead us by its most secret way following 'footprints on water' (*Dark Night* 1.II.17.).

It will lead us on a deep and hidden way within ourselves to the perfect union with God of a soul truly detached from all things because it is God's.

This is the perfection of prayer: union with God which becomes ever deeper and truer and so simpler, more natural and spontaneous. The soul is turned godwards and this affects all its actions and attitudes. It is not a brilliant light but quiet and sober. We may barely realise that it is there but everything is lit by it.

A living reality
And this is how prayer can become continual. It is an atmosphere in which we live. If we find it difficult to understand how we can follow St Paul's advice to 'pray without ceasing' isn't this because our idea of prayer is too 'artificial'?

We cannot keep up an attitude for long unless it is natural and spontaneous. The most natural and spontaneous movement of our deepest selves is suited to prayer. But because we have turned outwards and become caught up in many outward things, it is difficult for us to rediscover this cry to God hidden in our most secret hearts. We must in some way 'reconstruct' it, put the pieces together again and to do this we can use any thoughts and considerations which serve to reawaken the love of God in us. We must try and keep God in mind so that our hearts become accustomed to taking pleasure in him. But all this requires effort. Instead of being the spontaneous expression of our deepest selves, it feels more like a laborious artifact. Instead of being part of ourselves, expressing an habitual state of mind, it often feels like hard work. It feels like something we build outside ourselves which only stays up if we keep it up by a wearing effort. This is how our idea of prayer becomes 'artificial', in the etymological sense. We think of it as a construction, something we have made, not as something natural, the spontaneous expression of a vital instinct.

This does not mean that all our hard work is in vain. Of course it isn't! It only means we should remember that in spite of all appearances to the contrary, prayer is not something we 'build' from bits and pieces, something 'made by human hands', a work of 'art' resulting from our labour. This construction is and can only be a support or crutch for the living limb which must gradually regain its own strength. Or we can think of it as a building sheltering us through a long convalescence until our prayer becomes healthy, natural and part of ourselves.

This living reality is at the heart of all prayer. We should always remember that what is at the heart of our prayer is completely natural to us. (Of course we are not contrasting 'natural' with 'supernatural'. By natural we mean something spontaneous or even 'instinctive' – although in this case the 'instinct' is brought to life by grace.)

And in this way prayer can become continual, a habit. We shall see where its true perfection lies – in the truth of an attitude to God which has become really simple and spontaneous.

The heart of ourselves
The purpose of prayer is not to make us know the *object* of our faith better, to add to our knowledge. We can use knowledge as a means to our real end, which is to strengthen the hold of our faith. Our faith tells us that God alone is the only worthy object of our love and we hold onto him deep within us. We must constantly strive to hold faster. Deep in our prayer we must seek something that may be elusive and hard to grasp, but we know that among our heart's desires there is a deep longing truer than all the rest. It is not only stronger but different in quality. We cannot mistake it. This is the germ of life our prayer should develop and bring to maturity. We should care less about the blossom than the deep roots.

This is the pure faith which is at the heart of prayer and prayer's true perfection – from its first beginnings to its final end. If we find anything in us which truly and sincerely goes out to God, calling and seeking him, we have only to offer it to him trustingly. We must not bother too much about our feelings. We must not be astonished to find that this light is 'sometimes so subtle and delicate particularly when it is purer, simpler, more perfect, spiritual and deeper within, that the soul even when it is with it neither sees nor feels it' (*Ascent of Mount Carmel*, 1.II.14.). This soul knows that in its deepest self it loves God and belongs to him, that there is something in it going towards him. It lives simply in his sight and God in his love cannot fail to see the pure quiet light deep in the soul, a light which is simpler and more naked when it is deeper and more sincere.

This soul's deepest wish is for God. This is its prayer which never altogether ceases because it can never stop being what it is because of what it has in the depths of its being. The atmosphere it lives in is clearer and more peaceful because of it and it looks at God simply and honestly.

PART TWO

Meeting God

1. THE LORD IS THERE

The joy of his presence
We know that the Lord is there. We should welcome his presence as a gift.

It is a unique kind of presence because only he can come so close, so deep inside us that we can only find ourselves in him.

It is less important to grasp his presence with our minds than to submit our wills to it.

We should give him our consent in the night. This is true self surrender.

We do not know God but he alone can satisfy the longing in our hearts. These longings bear witness to him. We should believe by the simple assent of faith that the Lord is there. Our heart knows secretly what his presence means to us. At the least we have a foreboding of what it would be like if he left us.

However faint our apprehension of him, it is still the Lord. It is still his presence.

When we see the Lord our joy will not be entirely new. We shall recognise him who has been the joy of our life on earth. He will appear to us in the transfiguration of this joy. Our joy is the seed which contains this fulness.

God gives himself to us in a mystery of love. We should be humble in the face of this mystery and respect its secret. We should be simple. It is a mystery, a presence. Even when we do not know it we are taken up into the grace of this presence. We should simply believe.

Our faith in this presence is an absolute. It does not depend on the signs of it we are given. So we can welcome these signs in all freedom as and when they are given. And in this way we will be better able to recognise them, however slight they may be.

The signs are slight and in their very simplicity they invite us to respect the mystery and open us to its fulness.

The clearest sign of this presence is when it makes our hearts gentle.

We should accept what is deepest in our hearts without being able to understand. We live by it as if we were living by what someone else mysteriously brings alive in us. We must respect its silent action. We should recognise that it does not come from us, does not belong to us.

Freedom

The presence of the Lord in our lives is joy. In order to live freely with this presence we must learn to welcome it simply and gratefully as a gift.

We give thanks for this joy which truly gives us in all things the freedom of a happy heart.

We know that God's love protects us, so we should welcome everything that happens with serenity.

Our trust is in God's infinite love and knows no conditions or limits. It is an absolute.

And in others too we should only see the love God loves them with. Then our eyes will have the freedom to see what is good in them.

Someone is always there. Even when his presence is silent, every act of faith in him, even the bleakest, brings us to him.

We should let the silence come into our hearts in a secret apprehension of his presence.

We should live by the mystery of this presence even when we are apparently indifferent to it.

It is a gift to believe in it. This faith may be reduced to little more than an inability to give up seeking him.

Even if we are afraid that our inability to pray is caused by too strong an attachment to ourselves, we should believe that God always loves us and that we are in his hands. We should entrust him with our weakness, powerlessness and darkness.

Simplicity

We should behave simply towards him, believing in his love.

We may not feel his presence, but our faith in it brings us peace.

Even when we no longer know why we are at peace, we discover it in the depths of our hearts and we should welcome it.

Our hearts are imperceptibly caught up into the grace of his presence. His presence is always active. By living in this love's presence we become new creatures.

We feel this love in our lives every time it secretly but radically transforms them. This is where we meet God's love but we guess at what lies beyond.

What happens in our lives reveals to us beyond possibility of doubt that he loves us in our poverty.

We should consent to this poverty because we know that he still loves us.

We should try to live this love God loves us with as an absolute.

If we truly believe in it, we can only trust and hope in him. By welcoming it, we lay ourselves open to a love which goes beyond our awareness and takes us out of ourselves.

God's own humility is the only way we can understand the humility of prayer. God is ready to live with us, deep and close, on our own conditions in all their poverty.

We should live this life with the Lord in simplicity. Although the appearances are lowly, it is boundless life.

We should realise that we are living this mystery of love in our poverty, that we stand before him among the poorest. Then we will be able to recognise him in them. We learn not to doubt that he is present in this sinful world.

2. LIVING WITH HIS PRESENCE

Love ever active

It is a mystery that God loves us. We are completely taken up into this mystery. Nothing is left out. We exist only in it.

Even our faults and weaknesses are taken up into this love, and the grace of his presence.

What is deepest in us, what is most deeply ourselves, does not belong to us. If we lived at this depth and never forgot we had received it from another, we would be living really with the presence of God.

Why are we surprised if God's mystery reduces us to silence? And at the same time how can we fail to sense him infinitely near if we truly believe in him as a mystery of love?

When we realise that we could not be worthy of his gifts, then he will seem closer to us. We will recognise these gifts more freely and live with them gratefully.

The Lord is always at work in us. His love is ever active. When we see its effects this does not necessarily mean we see anything very definite or immediate. We must learn to discover God's more secret and gradual work. Our deepest attitudes change. We see things differently. In one way or another faith in God's love reaches the centre of all our attitudes, and we recognise this love as the primary reality. We should respect its mystery and its silences.

We should have confidence in what his mercy can make of our poverty.

It is deep and tastes of the infinite. It is delicate, we barely perceive it. By this we know that we stand before the mystery of God, present to us in the way our poverty makes possible.

We should learn to realise that we can encounter the Lord almost without being aware of it. And it may still be a real encounter.

However empty we may feel by accepting ourselves as we are we can always discern his presence in us.

Children of the Father

We are one with Christ who came so close to us in our humility. With him and in him we are loved by the Father. With him and in him we can share his fundamental attitude, the certainty of being loved by the Father.

In all simplicity we should have faith in his love for us. Through all the darkness.

In our very awareness of our poverty we can find the assurance that the Lord will not abandon us.

Our cry to God is sustained by all mankind's cry to him. We should try and believe more and live our belief more humbly.

God shows that his love is serious by the tests he does not hesitate to put us to in order to lead us to him, but he is not hard on the weaknesses of anyone who seeks him sincerely, humbly and in poverty.

This helps us to understand how the world as we see it can be the work of God's love, a love which takes our human response seriously but welcomes us in mercy.

A simple heart

God is present. We should realise that our faith in this presence is our own deepest truth. Apart from it, our self-awareness would only be an awareness of our empty nothingness. We should live by our faith in this presence. This is being in peace because it is being truthful.

We discover the Lord at the heart of our poverty.

We should be simple in the sight of God. This simplicity in faith should be an absolute.

Our hearts should be simple and resting in the Lord, liberated.

Knowing our weakness and the feebleness of our prayer should not lessen our hope but purify it.

We merely have an apprehension, but of infinite love.

Believing in God's love for us means living by it at the heart of our faith.

We live by his presence.

The more we believe in this love, the more we believe that it is ready to answer our faintest cry.

We express our faith in it by the simplicity in which we turn towards it, quietly accepting all our limitations.

It is a joy to be lived. Joy belongs to this love. It is a joy to know that in its omnipotence it can freely do what it likes with us.

The reality of the mystery

The Lord is ever present and active. When we pay attention we become more fully aware for a moment of an abiding reality.

The reality whose sign is the eucharist is always true. We are always in the presence of a mystery to which we must simply remain open, in faith.

The primary reality is the mystery which is the object of our faith. The slightest movement towards it is the movement of our heart such as it has gradually become in the Lord's presence, even if it remains hidden from us.

Our act of faith in God's love may seem weak and timid. It does not matter as long as we put our whole self into it. It remains at our own level.

We should try to find our hearts and give our consent to what they have become by the grace of this presence.

Our prayer should be very humble, a silence which the Lord can interpret better than we can. Nothing in this silence is hidden from him.

We should simply offer the prayer we are capable of at the moment. However poor it may be, it is what God wants from us.

Everything is contained in an act of faith in the fulness of the love God has for us.

If we truly believe in this love's fulness, we can be quietly content to remain with him, having only our desire to pray and our incapacity. We should truly expect everything to come from him, who is faithful in his love.

Faith is not something we feel. It is simply an inability to be sad or desperate because there is someone there.

Someone is there, however feeble our response to him, it is all the better an expression of our hope in him, if we simply stay with him in faith.

One day perhaps it will be given to us to see a bit more clearly who he is, who makes such behaviour possible.

Realising that we depend so totally on another, we find it impossible to judge anyone else.

3. THE LIVING GOD

What is most real in us
We do not need to see clearly what is in our hearts in order to offer it simply and with confidence.

We should peacefully believe that we are loved. This remains true even when we are apparently unaware of it.

What is most real in us is hidden deeper than our hearts.

We cannot guess its secret by doing violence to it. We need another way of seeing, which is discreet and above all acquiescent.

This acquiescence involves our will at its deepest level.

We acquiesce in faith. Our acquiescence is an act of faith.

We would like to pray with our feelings, but our poverty of feeling is a prayer which reaches our deepest self.

We should accept this poverty just as it is and put it in the Lord's hands.

Humble simplicity is the truest expression of what is most essential in prayer.

We should simply open ourselves to the Lord. We should believe in his action upon our secret hearts.

How can we not know he is present when we know well that nothing in us exists apart from him? We are penetrated by his presence. It is secretly but deeply and inalienably bound up with our consciousness of our selves.

Waiting and welcoming
We are in the presence of a love which asks only to give. This should be expressed in the simplicity of our cry to him.

We should not understand prayer as an effort to do God's work for him, but as waiting quietly for God and welcoming him.

We should wait and see what the Lord wants of us.

God loves us. He awakens the response in us and he can see this response better than we can. All our assurance is in this love and it alone.

We cannot doubt our response if we see it as the work of this love itself.

Our response is also a gift. We receive it from the Lord. It is the work of his grace. When we know this and live by it we truly become free and simple.

Our response is a welcome. We know that our welcome is imperfect but we put ourselves at God's disposal and offer ourselves to his grace.

We live in his sight knowing that he can see our faith in him.

We should be humble enough never to be astonished by our own poverty and confident enough never to let it become a reason for doubting that the Lord is present.

What is important is not what we are in our own sight but in the Lord's. We should stand before him in peace.

And something of God's way of looking at us, which we glimpse in this peace, should be reflected in the way we look at our neighbours.

Prayer is living an act of faith in which everything receives another dimension, nothing can be limited to what is visible but everything is open to something beyond itself where it can be seen in its truth.

Open to something beyond

We cannot doubt God's presence. We do not have to look for signs of it because it is the presence of a love in which we believe.

Our faith goes beyond itself by knowing that it ought to become even simpler and more confident.

In what we apprehend, we go beyond this apprehension, towards something beyond itself revealed in it.

Even if our faith is still weak it lays us open to a grace which is all-powerful.

Our faith in God's love is expressed in the simplicity with which we entrust him with our poverty, just as it is.

Our act of faith is also a choice. We chose this unique love, it may be nothing more than wanting to choose.

We should be sincere towards God and this means being open to him and letting him take what he wants.

When our awareness of our own poverty becomes more painful we should offer the Lord our trust that by his grace it may become more peaceful and a source of joy.

Lord, I would like this, I really would, and I offer you this because you know that I cannot yet do more. We are never sure of ourselves but we know well what we would like to be and that is what the Lord sees in us.

The assurance of faith

Our assurance rests not in what we have to offer but in our faith in him who receives it. We should learn to turn to him, even if it feels stiff and strange.

If we are aware of our own poverty and have no self-assurance – so that we cannot judge anyone else – God will not be hard on us, even though he is all-powerful and has the right to judge us.

We cannot go to God by an easy way which would allow us to be pleased with ourselves. We must go the way of humility, feeling the weight of our sin, which we share with our brothers.

Our hearts should be humble and meek, ready to receive the God of all mercy.

However wretched we are, prayer is being with someone.

We should simply live by faith our intimation of what is promised to us.

We can simply guess at it in the depths of our hearts and give our consent to it.

It is deeper than our hearts and it has become our very self.

It is beyond what we consciously apprehend. It is what the eucharist offers us, awakens in us and reveals the presence of in our deepest self when we receive it.

We should seek no other support than our act of faith. Our peace lies in this act of faith. This peace is always there and never alters, however much or little we may feel it.

God is present. We should constantly remind ourselves of his presence. It is our one reason for living.

We cry to him. He hears our cry and knows it is to him. We should consent to being deprived of everything because the Lord is always there.

We should be content with this and let him freely work in us. Even if his presence is unclear we lay ourselves open by our willing acceptance. In this submission we discover how deep in us his presence is. We should let him work on us.

It is not what our prayer is by itself that counts, but what it lays us open to. Knowing this is living with humility, faith and hope.

Persevering

We cannot reach true detachment by our own efforts. It comes from a presentiment of God infinitely beyond us and everything as nothing in his sight. We get this presentiment when we are praying badly but still feel the presence of a mystery which takes us up into itself. Our weakness is no obstacle to this mystery which does not have to be sealed down to it.

Prayer may have no tangible result. It may seem empty but if we really believe that we are taken up into the mystery of God's love, we will never be afraid of making too much room in our lives for an effort to pay attention to him.

4. 'WALK HUMBLY WITH YOUR GOD'

(Micah 6.8.)

The fulness of the mystery
Our humblest prayer opens us to the fulness of the mystery and we should place all our trust in it. Then our prayer becomes a pure act of faith.

Believing in God's love is also believing in what it has done in us and being able to recognise its work however weak the appearance of it may be. So great a love must be infinitely close.

Our trust is our evidence.

Our faith is not measured by our own strength but by God's in whom we believe. Faith goes beyond everything in us which is changeable and unstable. That is why we can live by this faith in freedom and simplicity, as a gift of grace – we simply give our hearts to it.

We look towards God with absolute devotion and trust. We look with love to God alone. We do not just glance at him in passing but keep him in sight in everything we do. The Lord can always see our attitude.

We should look to the Lord simply as we are, as we are in the grace of his presence. We offer ourselves to his love and mercy.

We allow him to be present. We give our consent to *him*.

Our living consent bears witness to everything he is for us.

The heart's silence
We do not clearly see or feel him.

We are aware of him in a different way. Our awareness comes from deeper within ourselves. We consent with our will and in so doing grasp something of what is happening. We become aware of our heart's deep desires which involve our whole being.

It is not like giving our minds to something on which we

reflect. It may be darker and barer. But we feel that it is also
qualitatively different. Instead of asking ourselves anxiously
whether we are really praying, perhaps we should simply ask
whether we are sure that our attitude is not itself a prayer.

The most important thing in prayer is the link we have with
Christ. It is a way of being ourselves in relation to him. And this
remains even when we are feeling bleak and empty and our
prayers express it badly.

Someone

We know that someone knows us. And does not this knowledge
also make us realise what he means to us? And knowing that we
are known is perhaps also becoming aware of our own deepest
truth.

In prayer the answer to all our difficulties is a simpler faith.
We must believe that the Lord in his clear-sighted love recognises
our prayer, even though to us it seems so poor a thing.

The greatest gift of God's mercy is prayer. In the presence of
the mystery of his love our poverty takes on all the fulness of an
act of faith in him.

When we realise this we cannot ourselves not be merciful.
We should stand in the Lord's sight in the joy of knowing that
this is how we exist. We are as his kindness sees us.

Grace

Believing in love is laying ourselves open to it, entering into·
communion with it. We can expect nothing more than the grace
to live in truth by this act of faith.

We know that we do not belong to ourselves and this sets us
free and allows us to live in an atmosphere of freedom, trusting
in God's love which wants us for its own and keeps us safe. If
we truly believe that our deepest being is by grace, it will be
easier for us to recognise that our simplest efforts are the spontaneous expression of what we truly are in the presence of Christ
who makes us one with him in his spirit.

We have nothing, we are nothing but what we continuously
receive. This dependence on the love which gives us life is our
deepest truth. Knowing this our very existence becomes a prayer.
We should simply give our consent to what is our own deepest
truth.

We should give our consent to God who is and remains heart
of our heart, in spite of all the apparent silences and emptiness.
We should keep coming back to prayer, knowing that we cannot

find anywhere else an answer to our deepest need.

Absolute trust

The more simple and trusting our faith, the easier it is to become aware of God's indubitable presence. He is present at the heart of our faith, in spite of all its darkness, and he demands our absolute trust. Our faith in God's presence in our lives does not rely on signs which in one way or another would lead us to put our trust in ourselves. Our faith rests in the revelation of the living God who is always present and whose mercy surpasses our weakness and cannot abandon us.

This is our basic attitude as christians which we have by our communion in the faith of the church. It is the deep instinct written on our hearts by the grace of baptism. It is what gives us our strength and stability. It enables us to live simply in the Lord's presence who has made us his by baptism.

It shows how deeply rooted is the attitude we try to have towards the Lord.

He who reads our hearts

God loves us and he sees the depths of our hearts. Prayer is offering ourselves to this love and letting it penetrate us. What we barely guess at in ourselves, God sees.

We should stand humbly in this love's sight, love which is also mercy. We should see God alone.

Our cry is completely simple because it is to infinite love. We aspire to him and appeal to him trustingly, even if we do not know what to make of our faith.

Humility is itself a welcoming attitude. We must put our trust in God alone. We must believe that the humblest prayer is taken up by his love's omnipotence.

Progress in prayer is learning to live more simply by pure faith.

We should simply live by our faith in what remains hidden from us. Faith is our assurance. In our feeblest prayer we should have confidence, not in it, but in God's love to which it gives us access.

We believe in *someone*. It is a person to person relationship. Faith's deepest truth lies in this simplicity and freedom.

The deepest and freest movement of our heart is towards God and we should trust him. He is secretly but intimately present in our very self-awareness. We can live by his presence almost without realising it.

Our prayer should be humble and modest, quite ordinary. It should be like the prayer of the poorest. Then it will be true.

If we find in our heart nothing but emptiness, this very feeling of emptiness is a need for God and a cry to him.

We do not need to express it but everything is in our simple act of faith and makes it deep, true and personal in God's presence. It is an apprehension of what he is to us.

We simply offer him our faith, however weak and hesitant. He welcomes it and gives it its full meaning and everything it lacks.

Faith is not something complete in itself. It finds its completion in a living relationship, an encounter. It is directed towards God in expectation. Our hearts can only guess but that is enough to be sure that the Lord sees.

A living relationship

God's presence is both manifest and discreet. We recognise it as our only good, but that it is not a good we can stretch out our hands for and grasp. The way we perceive his presence gives us a true attitude to it.

Our prayer should be a living relationship with him who takes us up into the grace of his presence. We cannot understand what we are doing when we pray unless we see it as an answer to what God is doing in us.

Prayer becomes itself in something beyond itself, in an openness towards God who is its hope. Prayer is not enclosed within its own limits.

We should believe that God's love hears what we stammer in our prayer. A more 'perfect' prayer might not be as pleasing to him.

We can find certainty in our faith by its free and peaceful recognition that God, what God gives us, is our one reason for living.

God with us

We do not set God at a distance by saying he is a mystery. He is also infinitely close and this too is an aspect of his mystery. As we penetrate the mystery of God we discover its simplicity.

Our faith puts us in the presence of a mystery which is infinitely beyond us but also infinitely simple. When our eyes are opened we shall see that the mystery was present in our faith in all the simplicity of its fulness.

If we really realised this it would purify our hearts. It would drive out from them anything incompatible with such a presence.

We should not think that God is far away because he is invisible. We find him in the relationship with him we have by faith. He is present to us in and through this relationship. As this relationship grows we grow in understanding of the nature and quality of this presence. We learn to live by it simply and peacefully.

Faith is not our work. It is a grace. Our simple consent lays us open to this grace and its hidden riches.

Answering

We do not know what answer we should offer God's love until we realise that our answer itself is part of this mystery of love. God himself elicits our answer, constantly.

We could give our answer very simply if we truly understood that it is also a work of his love in our hearts.

Our answer is silent. It comes from our humble faith.

We should not behave as if our cry to God was a way of forcing him to answer us.

5. THE LIGHT OF HIS PRESENCE

Meekness

Prayer is not calling to mind thoughts of whose truth we are convinced, so that we can make our feelings conform with them.

It is living by the attitudes grace has gradually created in us. We lay ourselves open to this grace simply by consenting to it.

Grace purifies our hearts and makes them peaceful.

Our prayer is only partially conscious. God who receives it in his love and mercy gives it its fulness of truth.

We realise our own poverty in this and so we cannot judge our neighbours severely.

We should not allow anything to shake our fundamental humility towards God.

Welcome

We exist by the welcome we offer to God. Our whole existence is a cry to him.

We discover that loving God means first of all being loved by him, at the heart of our love for him we discover his love for us, and so his love must become the primary reality to us and worth more than everything else.

God looks at us with all his love. Our humblest prayer acquires new meaning when we have some notion of what God clearly sees in our darkness.

We simply stand before God with some inkling of the mystery of his love and confidence in its fulness.

We should allow this love to set our hearts at rest.

We are happy, perhaps secretly, and this love is at the heart of our happiness. Our hearts are full and we give our consent.

We consent and our will remains in the light of his presence in which and through which we are and become all that we are.

Peace
If we are truly humble towards God we instinctively become gentle and patient towards our neighbour. This is the work of God's love in us and makes us unable to doubt his presence.

We want to find him in our hearts.

Grace awakens love in our hearts, a unique love of God and love of our neighbour. We should see everything in this love's light.

We should rid ourselves of anything that stops us loving, put it in the hands of the Lord and think no more about it.

We should open our hearts to God's love so that he gives them peace.

We should let him give us his peace. We should get rid of obstacles and let him work.

His presence should obliterate our all too human reactions. We should meekly accept what he works in our hearts.

If we truly love someone there is no need of forgiveness when he makes us suffer. Forgiveness does not come into it. We affirm that nothing can affect our love and that it can overcome the darkness. This is how God forgives us.

Consent
However great the darkness we should learn to discover God hidden beyond it. He perhaps very secretly fills us and weans us from everything which is not him. This world beyond us does not 'belong' to us, we simply lay ourselves open to its presence.

We believe in God infinitely beyond us, our faith is the work of grace. We simply give our free consent. Perhaps we give our consent in darkness, that does not matter. We must simply offer it and let his grace take it up. Grace gives it its true dimension.

If we consent and open our hearts to God's presence in them, this presence will not remain inactive. Gradually, secretly, everything we feel incapable of dealing with will give way to this presence.

Gradually we see things differently, the Lord leads us in communion with himself, into a new world. He teaches us to recognise his presence everywhere, to see everything in its light.

Seeing by faith
God's presence is hidden from us, but he is still close to us, if only we know he is there. We are close to him when we believe that he sees us and have faith in his presence.

In our prayer we get an inkling not of a far off mystery but of a personal presence we can only submit to.

We should be humble before the Lord and believe in the mysterious fulness of his active presence. Then it will fill us and give us peace, even when we no longer know whether we believe or not and we feel incapable of paying attention to it.

If our hearts become gentler we need no further proof of the Lord's presence.

There is a sense of the presence of God, a perception of his fulness which allows us to live by a pure act of faith, be it ever so weak. We efface ourselves totally before it.

Faith brings us within reach of the fulness of the mystery. It does not contain the mystery within its own limits. And so, secretly, it gives us the whole substance of joy.

We should not mistake this joy, we should know how to discern it, and learn to taste its pure sweetness.

The liturgy proclaims this joy continually. It makes all christians sing it.

A way to God is opened to us in silence. Our sense of his mystery, his fulness, becomes deeper as we realise he is our only hope. We efface ourselves in absolute trust.

The Lord reveals himself to us in silence.

Paying attention

We have faith in this presence. We express our faith by our consent and our humility before it.

The simple desire to pay attention to it lays us open to the grace of this presence and allows it to act freely in us.

Our whole being is taken up by this presence, it is our deepest truth, even if we are only dimly aware of it.

However poor our prayer, however apparently disappointing, it makes us live by faith with a reality infinitely beyond it.

We should simply try and reach a deeper self-awareness in order to discover what is never totally absent from us.

We should try to be what God sees in us. This is humility. Humility cannot be anything but a truthful attitude.

God makes us someone by what he sees in us.

We should humbly accept that the Lord's presence remains silent. We should allow it to give us peace. We should believe that it can give us peace, that its grace is more powerful than our resistances which so dismay us.

If we cannot conquer our feelings we should accept them in the sight of God. We should accept that God can purify us of all falsehood. We should give our consent to the secret action of his grace.

Everything we do to try and keep or re-establish communion in charity is true. Everything we do to try and satisfy the demands of self-love is false.

We should see others as God sees them. We should love them for the love God bears them.

We should live freely by our humble and trusting faith in God's presence which is a mystery of simplicity because it is a mystery of love.

Believing means adhering, consenting.

Everything in us is reduced to nothing before God's presence.

He who comes to us
If God wishes to raise his creatures to a communion with himself, he must do it in accordance with the demands of his love, otherwise it would not be a true communion.

But we must not understand the demands of divine love only in the light of his infinite holiness. Then it would be impossible to approach him, we could never be worthy.

God's love is the infinitely holy mystery of the communion of the trinity, but it is also the mystery of humility revealed to us in the incarnation. His love is infinitely close.

It hears our answer, even though it is given in our own poor language with all its imperfections, weaknesses and limitations. He takes our answer up into the fulness of his mystery.

Borne by his grace it becomes one with him.

How can we doubt the Lord's presence in our act of faith, when he has given us the eucharist?

God's mystery is simple, he is present in our humility. We should reflect his infinite mystery in our attitude to it. We should open ourselves to him and not try to enclose him within our own limits.

The Lord carries out his own plan in us. Our poverty is not an obstacle to him. Neither should we be dismayed by our inner emptiness and powerlessness. It is enough to know that the Lord is always there and always at work.

We offer ourselves to him by remaining silently before him. If we deliberately refused what we clearly saw God was asking of us, we would be going against the things in us which enable us to pay attention to his presence. We would lose sight of him, abandon him. We would realise how impossible it had become for us to live without his presence, however secret.

Novitiate Library

Closeness

We should no longer exist except by our openness to the Lord.

We should be nothing but this openness. Then we will only be able to see ourselves in him. We will learn to know him through everything we are. His presence will become the primary reality we recognise everywhere.

Encountering Christ in faith means forming a bond with him which binds us totally. We recognise him as our only hope. We discover his presence at the centre of this hope.

The Lord is present in our lives which we live in relation to him. Nothing is ours alone, everything is an expression of this relationship.

Knowing that we receive everything from the Lord, we know that he is present in everything that he himself brings to life in our hearts.

Everything in us is a sign of his presence, brings us into contact with its reality.

Everything, even the darkness. Because even in and through this darkness grace is at work, leading us to discover the truest answer we can give to God's love, the answer of faith.

Even in this darkness we must learn to recognise the presence of him who is carrying out his plan in us.

The closeness of this presence is beyond anything we feel, it is a mystery. What we are by the grace of this presence is not yet manifest but already 'we are called and we are children of God'.

However poor and empty we feel, we should see our lives by faith in the grace of this presence. We should believe in its power rather than our weakness. We should humbly offer it our desire to be obedient to it.

We can never be sure of ourselves, but we can be sure of God's infinite kindness.

The way to overcome any difficulty in prayer is always to trust him a bit more. A truly trusting prayer is always simple and serene.

6. OUR LIFE

Signs of God's presence
Simply believing in the Lord's presence and needing nothing else
but this belief is the way to welcome him really as a gift, humbly
and trustingly. This is the purest and truest way. Having faith in
the Lord's presence means recognising that it is our only reason
for living.

God's presence is inseparable from our deepest being. In it we
are all that we are. We can only be humble before it; we do not
possess it, it possesses us.

This presence is the primary reality. We cannot see anything
in us truly except in relation to it.

We should pay attention to this presence, but in a simple way –
not by trying to grasp hold of it. We must lay ourselves open to
it so that our deepest self is taken up by its grace in a way which
goes beyond our consciousness. We simply give our consent in
faith.

We are vaguely aware that this presence mysteriously fills us.
It is the presence of someone we know. We recognise his face
because we have lived with him.

We should not be surprised that what is deepest in us is also
most secret because it is more naked and pure.

'The road which leads to God is as hidden and secret from
the soul as is a road across water from the eyes. Tracks and
footprints make no mark on it; likewise the signs of God in the
souls he draws towards him by making them grow in wisdom
are also as a rule unseen' (*Dark Night*, bk. II, chap. 17).

Silence alone is enough to express a desire to pay attention to
him who is hidden at the heart of this silence.

The freedom of faith
We belong to God because we only exist by him. Our deepest

self belongs to him, our very self. When we become aware how absolutely we belong to him, and consent to it, we begin to realise how close is his presence.

'As the living Father sent me, and I live because of the Father, so he who eats me will live because of me' (Jn. 6.57.).

We are peaceful and have a joy with infinite horizons because of this presence.

The simpler our faith, the more completely trusting, the more freely we can open ourselves to the joy it reveals to us.

Our weakness and poverty is taken up by his grace and the Lord wants it to be by the grace of a close and intimate communion with himself.

The mystery of this union goes beyond all imagining; we can only adore it in the silence of faith. '... that they may be one even as we are one, I in them and thou in me...' (Jn. 17.22.).

In Christ we are taken up into the union which is the mystery of the trinity.

Faith is choosing deliberately to go beyond the darkness and hold on tight to the mystery. This is the right attitude. We should simply welcome the certainty we are given of what is the cause of our joy, in all its fulness.

We should simply and humbly welcome the assurance we are given that God is present and will never fail us. We must accept that by remaining a secret presence it is calling us to closer communion with it in faith.

We must believe in the love God has for us. Our faith is in him alone, not in ourselves.

We must lay ourselves open to what the Lord is doing in our secret hearts and accept that his work is hidden from us. It is his work, we should leave it in his hands. The measure of this work is his love.

We glimpse something of the truth of God's mystery by recognising its infinite simplicity. Its transcendent fulness is expressed in this simplicity. We too must approach it in simplicity.

We must accept that we can only express by our feeble cry what the Lord brings to life in us by grace deep in our hearts. It is still the cry of our whole being.

Faith is 'already there'

Seeing and knowing is one form of communion, but there is also the communion of faith. We meet the Lord in our act of faith because we recognise that it must be a gift of his grace that his presence penetrates it and gives it life. Our act of faith is our answer to his love. We open ourselves to him with absolute trust and thereby express that we belong to him alone.

'In this life faith is the mode of divine union, as in the next the light of glory gives the clear vision of God' (*Ascent of Mount Carmel* bk II, ch. 24.).

By faith we reach the mystery which lies at the heart of our faith. The grace of this mystery gives us our faith. By faith we are given to live by the mystery which will one day be revealed to us in light. Faith bears this hope in it, it is a pledge and promise that this hope will be fulfilled.

We should live humbly and simply by what is a gift of God.

The gift at the heart of a life of prayer is the grace of faith which enables us to live in the Lord's presence, however secret, silent and hidden this presence may be. We stop relying on ourselves and encounter this presence by realising we rely on God alone.

Our attitude to this presence should express our faith in it.

We should be all obedience, all attention.

We should respect the presence of the Lord in others. Nothing should prevent us from believing in it with a true and living faith. It is a mystery beyond our human limits and we should not allow these human limits to obscure it from us.

By recognising the presence of God in others, we learn to live freely in the joy of this presence.

God looks on other people with love. If we did the same it would radically alter everything. We would enter another order of reality, everything would acquire a new meaning, its only true one. We would feel we were discovering another world, which this present world we live in keeps hidden from us.

Open to God's presence

The primary reality which is the foundation of our prayer is the presence of the Lord. This presence takes up all our sincere efforts to pay attention to it and submit ourselves to it. However feeble our efforts may seem to us, they are true prayer.

In the grace of this presence all the struggles which seem so ineffectual to us become prayer.

We must believe in this presence and the power of grace by which it takes hold of us. It takes up our slightest move towards it and helps it on its way.

If we believe in the Lord's presence we entrust him with our prayer. We offer him our desire, the simplest movement of our heart and we know that his grace will work on them and lead them. This is the true hidden reality of our prayer.

The Holy Spirit prays in us.

His presence is very close and quite simple.

We turn towards the Lord because we truly believe that his presence is our one reason for living. This is sincere faith, not what we feel or experience.

There is joy in the bleakest and dryest prayer. This is the joy of trusting and it gives us peace.

If we are humble in our prayer, if we look towards God and realise that we receive it from him as a gift, we remain in the truth and in peace.

Prayer is openness, we must guess at what lies beyond it. We should recognise that our own attitude whatever it may be, requires the Lord's presence, and cannot be explained without it. Our attitude should be truthful. Thus it bears witness to God who is its cause.

We should learn to listen to the 'resonances' which even our simplest prayer sets up in us.

7. ENCOUNTER

Our deepest truth

What matters is that we are in the sight of God. God sees us and this is deep in our own self-awareness. In silence we cling to this truth. We need only apprehend it in order to cling to it.

We apprehend God in a deeper way than we are capable of putting into words.

We can freely live what is deepest in us without taking very much notice of it.

We know well that it is our deepest truth.

We live by it as a gift of God's love which we cannot doubt. Our unfailing support is faith in the love God has for us. Loving God is believing in his love for us. We love God by faith in the infinite fulness of his love for us. We see our own love in the light of his love, we love him with a love that reflects the fulness of his love.

Because to see him is to love him, let us no longer see anything but this love which we cannot doubt. Then we cannot doubt our love for him either.

Faith is more than receiving a word and recognising the truth of it. It is receiving from God's love the grace of believing in him. It is living our faith as a gift of love and this love is present in it and gives it life.

Everything in us should be seen in the light of this love. We should see it as a response to this love, awakened by it and supported by it.

If we try to love others unconditionally we understand better how God loves us. God's love comes before anything else; he loves us not because we are worthy but because he can make us worthy – and he is patient.

Love supporting our love

If we find nothing in our heart's silence, there is still the desire that the Lord should put in it everything he wants to find. We are at his disposal. We cry to him.

We cry to him knowing by a pure act of faith that he is near.

He gives us existence in his presence.

The harder we try to live by what faith reveals to us, the more difficult it will seem to believe it: that he who is so far beyond us is at the same time so close. But this is how we are in the presence of God's mystery and called to acknowledge in him a mystery of love which is beyond anything we can conceive. In the face of such a love we can never be simple enough.

The Lord's presence is a mystery. And the way it is revealed to our deep consciousness is also mysterious to us. We should not try to grasp it as we grasp something on our own level. The peace and joy of this mysterious love must be simple, secret and pure. It is transparent and may escape our notice.

We simply know that God looks at us with love.

We remain in his sight, entrusting ourselves to him. We must let his peace penetrate us.

The result of a life lived in the Lord's presence is a faith in this presence we may not even notice because it is so close to our own self-awareness. It can no longer be separated from it or be totally absent from it. We see everything in the light of this faith, even if we do not notice we do.

The humbler, more hidden and ordinary our prayer, the more it lays us open to the love of God because we trust in him alone.

He is our one reason for living and he is present throughout our lives. We give our acquiescence with our deepest self.

Freedom to love

Opening ourselves to grace does not mean trying to grab it, to see it plainly – it means consenting.

We give our consent to someone.

We look at him we love and have lived with, and the way we look expresses everything he means to us.

He can read in our eyes.

The Lord looks at us and we must humbly accept what we truly are in his sight. We put ourselves under his protection, with confident humility.

We recognise that our prayer does not belong to us, because what makes our silence a prayer is the way God sees us.

God is imprinted on our hearts and dwells in our silence even when we are unaware of it. When we know that God is looking at us this gives us some inkling of what is in the depths of our hearts.

In our silence we are open to the Lord. Our cry to him is a welcome.

We should not regard only our own weakness, as if we were alone. Its true meaning is in its relationship with the mystery to which it cries.

As we know we are in the presence of such a great mystery, we should not be surprised that we feel so inadequate. But when we recognise that in this mystery lies the fulness of love, we can have towards it the only proper attitude: simplicity.

Being simple means letting God see us as we are, and not bothering too much about how we see ourselves.

We look towards him and this expresses what we are in his sight.

We are not enclosed by what we are able to say in words about ourselves.

Praying is knowing that God loves us. His love for us is at the heart of our prayer. From God it receives all that it is in a pure act of faith.

The gift of faith

Faith is communion. The mystery it believes in is present in it.

We know we can only offer this mystery a welcome. And knowing this gives us an insight into the mystery itself.

The humbler we are in the Lord's sight, the easier it becomes to believe in his close presence, to welcome it as a gift of love which asks only to be received as a gift of love, totally free.

This love itself makes us worthy to receive it because it is so close to all that is humble and weak in us.

If we believe in God's love for us, we become free. Our freedom is adoration and thanksgiving.

Our faith is simple. We believe in Christ and our faith in him is a grace, a gift of his love.

Faith has its own unique certainty which cannot be reduced to any other kind of certainty. The certainty of faith is knowing that it is a gift of grace.

Our faith in God's presence is simple.

We must pay attention to this presence, humbly.

Our humility comes from our faith in God's love, and this love's light.

Our faith in Christ, our only support and assurance, is expressed in a simple and peaceful acceptance of our poverty in his sight.

We stand before the Lord not as we see ourselves but as he sees us.

We must have confidence that he looks at us with love.

If we humbly recognise our imperfections, he also looks on them with love.

The light of faith is the light which is Christ.

Our act of faith dwells secretly in our silence. We should seek nothing else at the heart of this silence.

8. LORD, TO WHOM SHALL WE GO?

Living communion

We must have faith in the love God has for us. We must have faith that God looks at us with love and makes us become what he sees. Our faith welcomes this love humbly.

Even when we feel nothing, faith remains. It does not need signs. It believes in what it does not see. It believes because it is sure of him to whom it is given.

Our will is the only obstacle to this love. Even if we are barely aware of God's presence we trust absolutely in his love.

We are made for this love. We have an inkling of this love in our heart of hearts. We cry to it and must simply live by it, however dark and imperfect our consciousness of it. We know that it goes beyond our consciousness. God's love is there, alive in us as a gift of grace.

We can only express what is deepest and truest in our attitude to God by a greater simplicity. We surrender in absolute humility, in the silence of faith which is open to the fulness of his mystery.

Our silence is respect for the mystery. We should not be surprised that this mystery reduces us to silence. At the heart of this silence lies the reality of a living communion.

We humbly live by this communion, believing in him we cannot doubt.

It is expressed in our attitudes, but never adequately.

Even so we feel something of the joy this communion brings.

Because we are sure of God, we have no need of signs. We can live freely in the light of this certainty.

Our certainty is our faith in the mysterious fulness of God's love. We know that we have entrusted ourselves to him.

His presence arouses our prayer. We consent. We listen to him.

Christ our light

God's love will always be infinitely beyond our thoughts. It would remain distant from us if we could not contemplate it in Christ. In Christ God gives us proof of his love, which remains a mystery, but a mystery expressed in things accessible to us. The mystery has a human face even though we still cannot bring Christ down to our own level.

If God had not taken on our own nature could we really believe that he invites us into communion with his own life, to enter truly into his own life of love? (Jn. 6 and 17.).

How could we believe we could come so close to him if he had not first become so close to us?

Only God made man could make us understand that he was inviting us to become so intimate with him.

Christ is the one object of our faith. He is the love of God revealed to us in its deepest truth and awakening our faith. It is a living faith which sees the face of him in whom it believes.

'He who has seen me has seen the Father' (Jn. 14.19.).

Believing means attaching ourselves to Christ and to everything which is revealed to us in him. This attachment is simple, deep and true. In all sincerity we can say to him: 'Lord to whom shall we go?'

Love is revealed to us in Christ in a mystery of humility. We are conscious of our own lowliness and we can believe in this love because it is also 'lowly'.

We should lay ourselves open to God's love giving our humble consent, in simplicity and peace. We know that he alone can give its full meaning to our act of consent.

If we truly believe in God's love for us, if we realise our nothingness in the sight of this mystery, our lack of feeling cannot cause us to doubt.

Absolute trust

If we turn in on ourselves, we become enclosed within our own limits. If we look towards God in faith in the mysterious fulness of his love, our desires and our hopes are open onto an infinite beyond.

We know that God loves us. We only exist in and by our faith in this love. We wait to know what he wants of us and we are satisfied. We ourselves have no wishes.

Faith is openness to the mystery, in all its fulness. Faith does not try to contain the mystery within any limits. Everything that comes from faith shares in this 'infinite' which is the object of faith. We attach ourselves to the mystery of the love God has for us, and the communion with himself he gives us. His grace takes hold of us and we reach the fulness of the mystery.

What opens us to the love of God is absolute trust. We surrender ourselves to God who receives us with his grace and mercy.

Love is being transparent to another. We have to give up our whole selves to it.

Our living communion is a mystery we only have an inkling of. What we guess at gives us the confidence to live by the mystery.

We know that God is always with us and sees into the depths of our hearts. In spite of darkness and emptiness we trust him.

However secret it may be, isn't there something in our own self-awareness which cannot be explained except by the presence of God? Isn't there something in us which looks towards him? Isn't our very humility an attitude towards God? God who is patient and merciful in his loving kindness?

We cannot confine God's infinite fulness within our thoughts. But our thoughts and attitudes could not be the same if we were totally ignorant of God. We are open towards God's infinity. We look towards him. We see enough to turn towards him.

Love comes first

The Lord is infinitely more anxious to give himself to us than we are to receive him. Rather than try to increase our longing for him, we should lay ourselves open to the Lord's own desire, by welcoming it more humbly, by putting all our hope in it.

God is love. Belonging to him means belonging to his love. We belong to him, knowing that he loves us, and putting all our hope in him.

At difficult times, regrettable feelings we cannot suppress makes us realise our weakness. But we can at least refuse to accept voluntarily such feelings as we see to be incompatible with our deep wish to go towards God alone. We must believe in the mysterious fulness of his love. We must try and be faithful. We should humbly entrust ourselves to him, without being dismayed by our own poverty.

When we are tired and feel nothing very much, we can rest in peace if we truly believe in this mystery of love which is all our hope. Our feeblest prayer can be a pure act of faith because we have no trust in ourselves.

May our faith in the mystery of God's love which enfolds us all in the fulness of its mercy always prevail.

Faith is born of love. Love is the way to truth; it make us recognise the truth. We believe in what we love. We pay homage to it by our love.

Faith is free. We trust God totally so we can be absolutely simple.

If our faith is true, it is enough.

We feel empty but we are open.

We are transparent and this gives us some idea of the light that shines through.

God's love is infinitely free to give itself. We must simply lay ourselves open to his love, and truly believe in it.

Although it is far above us, we have only to recognise that this love can satisfy our hearts and give us peace, and this is a way of expressing its infinite fulness.

9. GIVING OUR CONSENT

The infinite

God's fulness is present in the desire he awakens in our hearts. This desire can be satisfied by nothing less than the infinite.

In the light of this divine fulness we go beyond our own limits. Our hearts desire the infinite.

If we discern this desire, however vaguely, we recognise God's presence in ourselves and in others.

May we recognise the Lord's presence all through our lives. Let us remain open to the grace of this presence.

Believing in God's love is believing in the mystery of his love, but it is also believing in the loving relationship he wants to have with us. We recognise its presence in our daily lives. We know that we are entrusted to God who loves us personally.

We are open to the mystery and the mystery itself gives meaning to our welcome of it. In the face of the fulness of this mystery our welcome has to be completely simple.

If we truly believe in the fulness of God's love for us, our least act of faith, however weak it seems to us, will be full of hope.

We have faith in God's love, we respond simply. His grace which is a gift of this love, takes up our response.

Our hearts respond but we may not be fully aware of it.

Our act of faith finds its fulness in the measureless fulness of God in whom we believe.

'Love one another as I have loved you' (Jn. 15.12.).

We should try and love our neighbour with this love God has for us. In our prayers we have glimpsed something of the mysterious fulness of God's love.

Our true response to God's love is to love others. This is the best expression of our faith in him.

We should see every human being as someone God loves so much that he wants to share his life with him.

Faith is transparent

We should try to recognise in our simplest prayer the presence of the mystery we live by faith.

Simplicity is the proper attitude to have towards the presence of so great a mystery.

Pure faith looks towards God in simplicity and freedom.

We have simply to look to the Lord in faith and we receive the grace of his presence, in all its fulness. It bathes us in its light.

We look to the Lord and give our consent.

God is present and our loving relationship with him begins with faith and grows in the communion with him we have by faith.

We must try to understand the meaning of our act of faith, love expressing itself in faith.

God loves us and his love makes us exist only for him.

Our faith is a response to this love in simple trust.

We must have confidence in him who loves us in our poverty.

Faith is not our act alone. It is an exchange. In this loving communion faith receives its fulness and becomes an absolute.

We live by this faith and it is something more than all our efforts to pay attention to it.

Its light enlightens us even when we do not notice it.

It is a gift and a grace we cannot doubt.

Faith is a gift. By our faith in him alone the Lord gives himself to us.

At the heart of our prayer there is someone. What counts is our faith in him, in what he is, not what we feel or experience.

He is always in our hearts.

Living by faith in God's presence

The Lord is present at the heart of our act of faith. In spite of its humble appearances we live by the fulness of this faith which is constantly renewed by the sacrament of the Lord's presence.

We simply attach ourselves to him in faith.

If we live by faith in the Lord, we know that he sees this faith in our hearts, even when we do not.

May our feeble response never cause us to doubt the Lord's love. He loves us personally. May our weakness lead us to live by faith more humbly, and to a better understanding of gratitude.

If our faith in the Lord is true, we know that he will find it even in our silences. Then it is truly faith in him.

We must believe in the reality of his presence, which is always with us, towards which we can always turn, even if we feel nothing.

Turning to him means believing in him. It is an act of faith.

It is true prayer, humble and quite ordinary.

May our faith be simple free and true. Let us believe in the presence of omnipotent love which is ever active even if we only pay it intermittent attention.

Our faith is expressed in our desire. We want to lay ourselves open to him who can give us everything. We want to be obedient to him and let him lead us.

May we look to God with real faith. We have nothing but our trust in him we long for in the depths of our hearts.

This longing is most secret but also most strong. It is what is truest in us.

10. GLIMPSING THE MYSTERY

God sees us

We recognise what is deepest and truest in ourselves simply by paying attention to it and being it.

We are what we are in relation to another.

We are what we are in the sight of God, in the grace of his presence. God is our measure.

We can try to analyse what we are but there is something in us beyond analysis. We should simply live with it as a grace and a gift.

We cannot doubt God's presence and we know that his presence changes something deep in us.

We are sure that this something lives in us because we are sure of him who brings it to life by the grace of his presence.

We cannot leave God out of our self awareness.

If we truly believe in the Lord's presence, we will be able to discern the signs of it. however secret and silent they may be.

His presence is revealed to us by the faith in it which it arouses in our hearts.

We should trust God totally. We exist only by our relationship with him in whom we trust. This relationship is at the heart of our truest and most personal being.

We belong to the Lord, we only exist in him and for him. We depend on his love and are pierced through and through by his grace.

We should not trust ourselves but him in whom is all our trust. We remain in his sight.

God sees us in his mercy which is love and in his sight we should humbly be ourselves.

We glimpse in the action of his grace how he alters us.

If we remain in his sight, everything becomes possible.

The freedom of knowing we are loved
The Lord knows what is in our hearts. It is his work, the work of grace. He knows his own work, better than we do.

He sees us and in his sight we can simply be ourselves.

In our silence he finds a prayer we may not know about.

We offer him our silence. He gives us life and light.

He judges us, we should not judge ourselves.

We are free because we know we are loved. God's love can read our hearts better than we can. Our hearts should simply open to him. We should be content to know that we are what he sees.

We should be simply christian. Prayer has no other foundation than faith in the fulness of the grace of baptism.

We have faith in what Christ does with our lives by the grace of his presence. Our whole lives are taken up into the mystery of this presence.

We have given him our faith. Nothing can shake us. We are right to put all our trust in him.

We can always turn to his love. We need not be held back by the knowledge of our wretchedness, however great it may be. We have only to give him the freedom to do what he likes with us. We have only to let him make us obedient.

Nothing, not even our inability to respond, should allow us to doubt God's love. May we feel we are truly in the presence of the mystery.

Is there nothing in us which he could recognise as a cry to him, an earnest at least of good will? God awakens our response.

We should live by a very simple prayer, believing in the mystery which it opens to us.

It is joy to live by receiving what we are from him in whom we are all that we are. We discover him in all that we find at the heart of ourselves.

A clear-sighted love
We must let the power of grace act on our weakness. Our weakness should become a welcome and awareness of this power.

We should lay ourselves open to this power, by which and in which we are all that we are.

At the heart of our prayer lies our faith in him who is always at work even when we do not know it.

When we wonder if he is still there, this means we are seeking him. We lay our heart open to him simply by seeking him. He is at work in secret.

Faith begins with trust. If we place our trust in God alone, we go some way into the mystery of the fulness of God's love. We discover this fulness by becoming aware of its mysteriousness.

He who is entrusted to God's love is free. God's love is clear-sighted and sees in our freedom the purest expression of our trust in him.

Our faith is the truest thing about us. It is present simply and spontaneously in our self-awareness. It is a grace and gift.

In everything that it is, faith is faith in someone. We turn towards him who can read our hearts. Faith lives in freedom and simplicity; it is not turned in on itself.

If we truly believe in the depths of God's mystery, faith must always come first. It will lead us to recognise gratefully the fulness of the gift we are given in this unspectacular way. The divine mystery we know by faith in the eucharist under the form of bread and wine, is also always present in the form of humdrum daily life. It is present too at the heart of the most secret and silent prayer.

As our hearts open to faith in this ever present mystery, our lives become a prayer.

We should open our hearts to this faith, so that it may free us from ourselves and make us belong to God alone.

Beyond all measure

In us God loves himself. He makes us one with himself, and gives us by grace a true share in the loving communion which is his life. And there he loves us.

He is wholly present in the love he gives us.

He truly gives himself to us in this love.

If we look at things from the point of view of our own little-ness, we dare not believe that we could receive so much, and what we are taught by faith will not be living truth to us. But from God's point of view, in the fulness of the mystery of his love, nothing can surprise us and we accept his word in all simplicity. The better we believe in the fulness of God's love, the better we understand that we can only live by it together.

We should accept faith as a grace, as it is given. It lays us open to the fulness of the mystery. It gives us a glimpse of what God can do, although we cannot.

God's love is infinitely free to give itself, and infinitely able to awaken a response in our hearts which it can interpret. It is able to recognise the love we express by the humility of our welcome.

Faith lays us open to the mystery. Our faith can be present and real even though our hearts feel empty.

We should try and express our faith in our lives. If we truly believe in the presence of so great a mystery, we must also recognise it in other people and only see them in its light.

We stand before the infinite, the infinite fulness of love. We receive from it our very response to it in absolute simplicity.

Trust in God should come first.

The Lord is not present to us only as someone is present when we are thinking of them. He is really present in everything which he himself brings to life in us, in every movement of our hearts. We must respect the mystery of this presence.

11. THE FULNESS OF THE MYSTERY

Freedom and trust

We cannot feel or experience anything adequate to this mystery.

God alone can reveal it to us. We can only receive it in an act of faith in his word. Nothing can touch this faith.

The darkness in us detracts nothing from it.

We can only see something of the meaning given to our lives by this great mystery. We must believe that it is present in our humdrum daily lives.

We should not be dismayed at the simple manner in which we are asked to live by faith.

We should live by faith in humility, a joyful and confident humility which opens the way to love.

Our faith in God's love for us is a source of peace and joy. We should accept this joy as a gift of love. Even if it is a very secret joy, living with it is living in a loving communion.

At the centre of our joy there is a presence.

What better way is there of approaching the mystery than by recognising its fulness? We should not be surprised at our own smallness in comparison. Perhaps the poverty of our welcome is the truest thing about it.

We should open our hearts to the desire God himself puts in them.

We should offer our hearts to him and humbly try to do his will.

It is not our awareness of the gift we receive that is its measure. This would confine it within our own limitations.

The measure is our welcome. We offer our emptiness as a silent appeal.

God is at the heart of our humility and we welcome him.

We know our poverty and offer it to God's infinite fulness

which alone is able to make us want him and supply that want.

If we truly believe in God's love, we believe that even silence is a cry to him when we have nothing else. God sees our faith in it. He takes it up by his grace. We should not try to confine this grace within the limits of our own hopes. God is the measure.

Every slightest movement towards God is an act of trust which enables us to escape from our limitations.

Anything in us that might stand in the way is set aside when we set ourselves aside in the presence of the infinite mystery of God given to us by faith.

We know that by faith we are taken into the presence of God who is ever active. God comes before our faith which makes us aware of him and live with his presence.

Faith's infinity

If we truly believe in God's love, nothing can surprise us. The mystery remains a mystery, but it is now the mystery of the gift of infinite love by which God gives the whole of himself to us.

The sign and the pledge of this gift are the incarnation and the eucharist.

We are silent before the mystery as we contemplate its fulness. Our faith in it goes beyond all the limits we might be tempted to set on the possibility of so great a love coming so close to us, entering into communion with us.

In the presence of this mystery the meaning of our response becomes clear. It always is a response. God loves us and enables us to welcome his love. God inspires our act of faith. He is present in it and enables it to go beyond our limitations. We are silent and God's presence is a secret influence. We have only to believe and we remain in contact with it.

In faith we recognise the presence of Christ in others, even if it is as hidden from us in them as it is in the silence of our own hearts.

In the depths of our silence there is an act of faith, which can be pure faith.

Living by faith is living in a loving communon.

The taste of pure water

Faith is at the centre of our self awareness, and makes it what it is even when we are not thinking about it. We believe in God's love for us. We should learn to discern it.

Believing in what we neither see nor feel is a source of peace and joy which tastes of clear water. We should recognise this joy and welcome it as a gift of love.

It may be a secret joy but its measure is the love in which we believe, in all its fulness. This joy enables us to live in God's love.

However feeble our prayer it truly expresses our love of God if we cannot live without it.

If we truly believe in the fulness of this mystery of love, we know that we have only to open our hearts by the slightest movement towards him and he will work on us in his omnipotent freedom in which is all our hope.

The joy of his presence is constantly renewed by the gift of the eucharist.

We should see our neighbour in the light of our faith in God's love, that is we should above all be loving. Love comes first and is unconditional. We see everything in its light and nothing can shake it.

We truly see things differently.

Believing in love means believing in the new life it gives us, even if this new life in the grace of God's presence is very secret.

God's love awakens our desire and satisfies it. It leads us in silence to the only true meeting place with him. We meet him at the heart of our act of faith in him.

Perhaps our faith is still weak. But if we live by it simply and humbly, just as it is, we open our hearts to grace.

God knows our weakness and wishes to manifest his power in it. Perhaps this very weakness makes faith really itself. Perhaps this weakness leads to a true meeting with the Lord.

Already and not yet

Silence is itself faith in God's presence and an unwillingness to be distracted from it.

We offer this silence to the secret influence of his presence.

If we truly believe in God's presence we do not need signs. Our silence itself is an act of faith.

Because God is present our silence is not empty.

Faith is a welcome. We attach ourselves to God and give him our consent.

Faith gives us access to what we do not see. It enables us to live by what we cannot yet see.

We should not belittle the greatness of our vocation. God is great and he wants us all to share in the mystery of his love. Everyone who shares in this communion will have fulness of joy.

When we are welcomed into this communion we receive the whole of it as a gift of love.

True charity is a foretaste of this joy that is promised us.

The joy to come is already there in charity.

We should believe that God in his love who puts this longing for him in our hearts cannot then fail to respond to it. He sees our desire even if we are silent and weak.

We truly meet the Lord and live by his presence simply by our act of faith. Our act of faith in his word recognises the presence of the speaker and the gift of himself he offers us.

Joy we barely perceive can still be very deep. It can express our love for him whose presence is our only good. We gratefully live by his presence.

We can only overcome our darkness by a firmer faith in God's love for us and by living it more simply.

Consenting to a gift

God is present to us in our own deepest self. In our whole being transformed by love we discover him we love.

By loving him we have become what we are. We can now only see ourselves in him.

We must simply consent. And our consent offers us the infinite, the grace of God's presence.

God's presence may be revealed to us by a change in our selves we barely notice. It is only when we are distracted from this presence that we notice something missing. A spark of life has gone out and we are left in darkness.

Our faith in God's presence should be absolute enough to be lived in all simplicity. We should not be dismayed by any silence.

We know that God will not go away even if in spite of our selves we still resist him. Gradually he will overcome our resistance. We should open our hearts to him and trust him.

We should live quite simply by the presence of God whose love is our one reason for living. We know that he precedes any movement we make towards him. He pushes us to reply to his call.

We offer him these movements just as they are. He asks us nothing he does not give.

We cannot doubt the Lord's presence in our silence, once we humbly live by it and welcome it as a gift.

We must respect the mystery that dwells in our silence. It is the mystery of God's infinite love for us. We should be humble towards it.

In simple trust which expresses all he is to us, we stand before him.

We turn freely towards God knowing that our every cry to him is received by his omnipotent love. Our humble move towards God becomes an act of faith and trust.

We stand before him as what we have become by the grace of his presence.

In order to believe that God loves us, and how much he loves us, we must realise that his love is absolutely free.

We should not think we deserve it.

We should recognise that we have nothing we have not received. But we have received it and we go on receiving it. God's love does not humiliate us but raises us to his level. We humbly welcome his gifts and our welcome is a communion.

12. THE STRUGGLE FOR FAITH

We must not doubt God's love
The love which is deep in our most secret hearts makes us want to keep turning to the Lord, even if he always seems to be silent.

We are all that we are in and through his presence. We find his presence in our own attitudes, deep within ourselves.

His presence is a free gift. We should welcome it as such in lucid simplicity.

His presence is our only good. We receive everything from it. It transforms us little by little into its own image.

We have only to believe, with a true act of faith.

Giving our faith means giving ourselves.

We know that anybody who does not deliberately cut himself off from this presence will be satisfied by it beyond all his hopes and wishes.

If this is part of our faith in this presence, then we truly believe in it.

Our hope is in God alone, in his infinite love. That is why nothing can destroy it. It is stronger than our own selfishness. As we realise the fulness of the mystery of this presence, our faith in it becomes simpler and more alive.

We put all our hope in God and surrender ourselves to him.

If we doubt what is living in our hearts, we are doubting God.

We are doubting that God is infinite love which gives itself to anyone who does not refuse.

Our trust in God can never be simple enough.

We can doubt an idea or an abstract notion. We cannot doubt a person. We cannot doubt love.

However tired and empty we may feel, the Lord is there. He dwells with us. We must believe in him always.

Because he is present, we are not just empty but open. We hope and our faith is expectant. Our humility is joyful and peaceful.

He who comes to us

However poor our prayer, it is the Lord who makes us pray. We should know that he is present in this humble prayer and that it comes from him.

We should simply live by the love God gives us for himself. We should believe in our love for him as a gift of his love for us.

We believe because we believe in his love for us.

We should not fail to recognise this gift hidden in our prayer.

We must learn to appreciate its secret fulness.

A peaceful heart without desires is satisfied.

If we lack nothing, this is because we have everything.

Why should we want another way than this which leads us to a realisation of God's greatness in humble and trusting simplicity.

Humility does not mean lowering ourselves. Our true greatness lies in being aware enough of God's love for us to be able to live simply trusting him alone and not being surprised by our own weaknesses.

Our faith in God's love for us answers all our questions.

We know how feeble is our response, but we believe in his omnipotent fulness, There is no common measure between the two.

We do not believe by a faith which comes from us, which would be at our level, but we lay ourselves open to the grace, constantly renewed, of believing in God's love as a gift from the Lord.

If we welcome God's love as a gift we accept it in freedom and simplicity and without self-regard.

We should have a child-like simplicity. The child's parents are thrilled by the simple and trusting way it looks at them and by its behaviour, even though the child may not know it.

We should be like God's children.

Any prayer is a true prayer if we offer it to the Lord's mercy and ask him to make it a prayer.

We realise our weakness before God because we want to go to him. Our weakness is a cry to him.

Whatever we may feel, it is enough if these feelings are in one way or another a need for God, an openness to God. He alone can come to us.

In everything we do we should expect everything from the Lord.

Humbly and obediently we should let him lead us. Our humility should be an act of thanksgiving.

If we do not see clearly, if we are afraid we are not really honest with ourselves, we should ask God for light. He will not refuse us if we ask him for it sincerely.

Boundless love

The best place to meet God is in our act of faith. This act of faith is simple and deep. It is deep because it is faith in such a deep mystery. It is simple because of our humble state.

We should recognise the presence of the mystery in our act of faith and we should not be surprised that we live so simply in this presence. It is the mystery of God who is love, the mystery that God loves us.

However poor and clumsy our prayer may be, the Lord can make something of it.

In the prodigal son returning because he was hungry, his father simply recognised his child. In us too, however we may come to him, God recognises his child.

We should go all the way in our faith in the fulness of this omnipotent love. Our faith must be pure enough to remain peaceful when we feel quite empty inside. We should not seek any other support.

For our prayer to be really prayer, only one thing is necessary, that we remain truly humble in the presence of God.

Faith works a mysterious change. God alone knows the secret of what he brings to life by the grace of his presence in a heart which is open to him.

The secret of this communion is not yet revealed to us, but neither is it completely hidden. He in whom we believe is present in our faith.

Our faith is directed towards his infinite fulness and has no limits. Faith is the apprehension of infinity.

Faith is love and the apprehension of love. It is an apprehension of boundless love.

God's love has no limit. It does not calculate. If we open ourselves to his love we open ourselves to the limitless freedom with which God gives himself to anyone who is prepared to welcome him.

We should let God open wide the door which we ourselves can barely open a crack.

We should turn towards him with joyful trust, boundless trust. In the silence of our hearts we should believe with our whole soul. We should set no limits on our faith in God's love.

We should quietly offer our wants to God who foresees them and will supply them. He satisfies them in advance.

We should also offer him our desire to want him more.

Our only support

We believe in the Lord and have faith in his love. This means knowing that even if we have nothing, if we do not know what has become of our faith, he is always there holding us by the hand.

When everything has gone, God remains. He is always with us and he sees in the depths of our hearts what we can no longer see.

Everything rests on the word spoken to us in Christ. He is the one word of the Father, in whom the Father reveals himself and what he is for us. This word is our one support and it will not fail us. Our faith in this word is backed by the faith of the whole church. It is revealed in every encounter with Christ in the eucharist. Our attachment to this word is the result of the patient work of grace which reveals to us the full meaning of our act of faith. It is a gift which remains in our most secret hearts even when it seems that everything has gone.

The mystery is ever present. It does not depend on our awareness of it. We are laid open to its grace simply by giving our heart's consent.

God's love is infinitely clear-sighted. He can see the slightest movement we make towards consent, even if we do not see it.

We should humbly offer what we know will be accepted.

By our consent we become at one with what grace brings to life deep in our hearts, beyond our clear knowing.

We become peaceful inside. Worry and self-regard disappear because our trust in God is absolute.

We should believe that God's love is free and that we can expect everything from it.

We should remain in God's presence. His love always goes before us.

We should lay ourselves open to him in peaceful trust and try to become obedient to him.

God's love is never inactive. Our faith in him should be an openness to the constantly renewed grace of communion with him.

13. A HEART SECRETLY SATISFIED

Love casts out fear
We must open our hearts to love and welcome it. The more we welcome love, the more truthful will be our attitude and the more open our hearts.

We must not try to force God's hand. We cry to him believing that he wants to give himself to us.

We should try and become obedient to the demands of love.

So great a love should make us want to come ever closer to it, to belong to it more completely. Our desire for God has no limits because God's love has no limits. Only our trust in God's love can satisfy this desire.

We trust in him and feel confident that he can satisfy our desires. We simply remain open knowing that someone is waiting to come in.

Because God loves us with so great a love, we should have no anxiety. True faith in God's love would set our anxiety at rest, even the anxiety that we might not have the right attitude to God.

God is infinitely capable of opening any heart which does not wilfully shut itself off from him.

We may feel inadequate in the sight of this love, but knowing that we have entrusted our inadequacy to God is itself a close bond with him.

By faith we see God's love as infinitely beyond us but also infinitely close. By faith we apprehend the mystery of a beyond which is not far off.

We should have total faith in this mystery. Our faith should let in its light and God should be all in all.

Whatever gleam of light we may have seen remains with us even if night comes again. We remain in peace when we know this and believe it.

We should recognise anything, anything at all in other people, which shows they cannot live without God, that there is something in them which cries to him. We are not alone in feeling this, so the feeling is not an illusion. What we recognise in others confirms us in the truth of these feelings.

Humble love
God sees us. We stand before him and he looks at us lovingly. We should stand before him as he sees us, just as we are by his grace.

The Lord looks kindly on anyone who recognises his own poverty in God's sight and puts all his hope in God.

We should seek nothing except what makes us behave more humbly towards God. We should try and deepen our humility and give it meaning.

Faith is humility. It is a loving humility.

It is the humility of recognising the presence of God's love for us in our own humble state.

The mystery is revealed by the faith in it which it awakens in our hearts.

Humbly, lovingly, we belong to God.

We should know that the Lord sees us, his love is always at work in us and we can be peaceful in his sight.

The mystery in our lives is the mystery of a living and active presence, a personal presence.

We should let our hearts go where they want, even if we do not know where they are going, because we know that God leads them by his grace.

We should discover the presence of God and live by it in humble faith.

We should surrender all that we are to the Lord, because he alone made us. We should have no desires in his sight.

We should be all faith and love.

Perhaps we barely feel this peace but we apprehend the infinite from which it comes.

We should keep silence so that we become conscious of our deepest truth, what we are attached to in the depths of our hearts.

We are attached to God and we know that if he went away we would have no reason for living.

We know that we have only him and that everything we have is in him.

The whole fulness of God's love and mystery is present in the simplest of gifts we constantly receive from him day by day. He offers them to us with all his love, even if the gift is sometimes a test.

We should be at peace through our act of faith in this love.

God is present even in our silence and our weakness.

His love bears us in his grace even when we do not realise it.

We should simply pay enough attention to the presence of God to make sure that he governs our attitudes and our own self-awareness.

He is present and we know that we can trust him absolutely.

Our trust is infinite, in God infinitely beyond us.

We can never believe strongly enough in his love.

Our act of faith itself makes us humble.

The truer our faith the more it goes beyond itself. Nothing exists except the fulness of the mystery of love, the infinite freedom of this love, which is the object of our faith.

The eucharist is the fulness of the mystery made present, manifest in the act by which this mystery is given to us in its totality.

A secret grace

Faith is not a merely human attitude. It is a gift received at baptism, sustained by the grace of the Spirit who dwells in us. It is a secret grace which we must live by in simple trust.

Faith does not dispel the darkness, but it offers us a secret fulness beyond all the darkness, which we must learn to live by in peace – learn to receive.

We should live simply by our faith. We know that it is the deepest thing in us. It bears witness to something beyond us. He who is the object of our faith sees this faith in our hearts.

Faith is what is deepest in us. Through all the silences we know that we possess everything, in spite of our poverty, because we can trust God's love for us.

Our faith in his love should be an absolute. Even when we are unfaithful, the Lord loves us. He leads us back to himself.

If we truly believed in his love we would believe that it is always at work. Our silence would become an openness towards this love. We should not need signs.

However poor we are, the Lord is at work in our poverty. Gradually he establishes in us a humbler and purer faith in him alone.

Faith and self-surrender mean not trusting in ourselves but putting ourselves in the hands of another. We accept the darkness, knowing that someone else sees clearly for us in this darkness.

Joy already given

Our humble prayer, peaceful in spite of our poverty, should be an act of faith in God who receives it.

Any prayer is true if it is an act of humility trusting in God alone.

At the heart of our act of faith we glimpse the mystery, because we cannot approach it except by this act of faith.

Our heart is in harmony with the joy of heaven, for which it is made. It longs for this joy. It has a foretaste of it in the life of faith. This joy gives truth to our prayer.

We meet God deep within ourselves, we know that in him and through him we are all that we are. We are not before him, we are in him and he in us.

We must remain open to the mystery of his presence. We recognise it in the peace it brings us.

As we apprehend the greatness of the mystery in whose presence we are, we realise that the truest prayer is the most simple, humble and modest.

This simplicity is all adoration.

God himself who dwells in us gives us this attitude. It is not our own. When we have this attitude we no longer belong to ourselves.

We long for God and welcome him with our whole self. We know that we will not be disappointed because we trust his love.

Our longing is not anxious, as if it belonged to us. We express our longing by our humility.

True freedom

A greatness which keeps people off is a limited greatness. It is imprisoned in itself. God's greatness has no limit. It is infinitely free, and therefore infinitely simple.

The simplicity of our prayer is an act of faith in the simplicity and infinite freedom of God in whose presence we are.

If we truly believe in God's presence, we will be ready to carry out what God begins in us. We welcome God in a communion.

We can no longer live alone. We are open to God.

God is always with us and cannot be taken away from us. We believe in his love for us.

If we truly believe in his mercy, nothing can make us doubt his love.

Because God loves us, our act of faith, however feeble, means something and is truly a prayer. God receives it in his love and completes it.

We should simply be what we become in the presence of the Lord, what he makes us become by living in a daily communion with him. This is our deepest truth, our deepest self.

Everything that is in us only exists in and by his presence, even if this presence is a secret presence.

We simply look towards God. We become humbler and our humility becomes truer as it becomes more confident. We look towards the Lord and he sees what is in our eyes.

All our security comes from him in whose presence we are. He loves us and can interpret our silence, knowing that it is a cry to him. He can see in his mercy what is hidden from ourselves in our own hearts.

We have nothing but we know what God makes of this nothingness.

We put all our trust in him.

'With you, I am'

The measure of prayer is God's love, not the prayer's own quality.

The goal of prayer is not what we reached by our own limited efforts.

The goal of prayer is the infinite mystery which takes us into its own fulness.

Our prayer is always an openness to the mystery. It only has its being in and through this mystery.

The Lord is present at the heart of our faith. Our faith leads us beyond what we see.

In our deepest being we have a bond with God which cannot be broken without destroying ourselves.

Our whole being is centred on this bond which is truly present in us however secret it may be.

Our attitude towards God is not one among our many attitudes but at the heart of them all. Without God's secret presence in our very self awareness we could not be what we are.

We know that we are loved, a mysterious love. When we recognise its mystery we see something of its fulness.

We trust in him and he takes our trust beyond itself.

Our trust leads to true freedom in our prayer.

Even if our prayer is weak like us, God's omnipotent grace is present and active in it.

Our most personal being only exists, can only be truly itself in relation to another and in communion with him.

We should live meekly in this communion.

We should offer God, who sees everything in his infinitely clear-sighted love, what we can only guess at in the depths of our hearts.

We offer simply our deep need not to be separated from him,

whose presence is everything to us, even if it remains hidden and silent.

When we are near him we begin to feel the joy of his presence, a pure, clear joy we welcome in faith. This joy opens infinity to us. We cannot doubt it because we cannot doubt him who is our joy.

Faith is love

We should make space within us for God's presence, for the grace of his presence.

Our prayer is simply an openness to what God in his mercy works in us.

We entrust our silence to his love.

We have the boundless freedom of a hope which is faith in his love.

We belong to this love and should let it do what it wants with us.

It is our only good. We do its will, not ours, and so express God's love for us.

Our only good is to do God's will, not ours, and to express his love for us.

As it is our only good, we cannot confess it better than by entrusting it to the Lord.

Absolute trust is a fundamental christian attitude. It is the expression of the faith we received by the grace of baptism.

We trust God absolutely, even when everything is silence. Then silence becomes a prayer which we know is heard.

Our faith is clear. The mystery it believes in is present and very close. This presence makes our faith an absolute, in spite of the darkness.

We should humbly accept the gift of faith just as it is given to us, in all its darkness.

We should recognise the peace which is the fruit of faith, deep in our hearts.

We live by this faith and we know that it cannot rest on emptiness.

It is a living certainty and brings a peace which tastes of the absolute. Doubts cannot reach it.

It is an incredible mystery. God loves us. He does not ask us to believe but to live with it. Believing it can only mean living by it.

We must love the poorest people, in order to understand that God loves them, in order to understand that there is something lovable in poverty. Then we can feel that God loves us.

God cannot but be merciful to anyone who humbly recognises his own poverty and entrusts it to him.

Because we cannot yet see God, God could only give us faith to approach the fulness of his mystery without confining it within our limitations.

Faith is first of all a grace which can only be welcomed in humility.

Our faith should be humble enough to accept any darkness.

We should give our consent to God's love for us. We consent to belong to him alone. He can treat us as his. Even our consent is not our own, confined within our own limitations. We offer it to his grace.

What we shall be

We have faith in a mystery which is already given to us.

We apprehend the mystery before we die. But the mystery by which we have lived, perhaps not very successfully here on earth, expands in heaven into the vision of God. In the light of this transfiguration our earthly life acquires its true meaning.

The mystery God offered to us on earth in his mercy is now revealed. We see God. All the blessed will be united in this fulness, because they will all share in it. This unity will overcome everything that might divide us.

This shows the spirit in which we should live in the communion of saints here below.

We should see our neighbours as sharers in this mystery. In them the grace of this mystery is offered to us. The people we meet are part of God's plan for us. They are part of our history, in which God works out his plan for us.

May nothing divide us and damage this fundamental unity, may nothing prevent it from being a help and a comfort.